"For parents, watching their young ones navigate the often bewildering experience. *What is going on in those act the way they do? How can I help them grow to their full potential?* In *The Emotionally Intelligent Child*, authors Katz and Hadani reveal the inner workings of the child's developing mind and offer parents useful techniques to help their children become more caring, thoughtful, and emotionally balanced."

—**Neil Izenberg, MD**, founding editor in chief of Nemours www.kidshealth.org, professor emeritus of pediatrics at Sidney Kimmel Medical College, and advisor to organizations dedicated to children's health

"Rachael Katz and Helen Hadanis' marvelous new book, *The Emotionally Intelligent Child*, will bring instant clarity and calm to parents who are struggling to help their children navigate social dynamics and turbulent feelings. Readers will feel that two knowledgeable and skillful experts are holding their hands and walking them through just the kinds of crises and dilemmas all parents face."

—**Susan Engel**, senior lecturer in psychology, and director of the program in teaching at Williams College

"As early childhood educators and parents, Helen and Rachael have a deep understanding and respect for the internal workings of children's minds and children's emotional development. They bring a smart, practical, and unique perspective to understanding and nurturing children's social and emotional growth. This book is a must-read for parents who want to give their children the internal tools for success in school and beyond."

—**Karyn Flynn, MBA**, former CEO of the Bay Area Discovery Museum; and founder of Holos, a weekly newsletter

"There is nice- to-know information, and then there is need-to-know information. *The Emotionally Intelligent Child* is a must-read book for parents and caregivers looking for need-to-know information and strategies as a guide to raise socially and emotionally intelligent children."

—**Solwazi Samuel Johnson**, mindfulness teacher, and mentor

"You 'had' me from the very beginning! 'Raising an emotionally intelligent child involves seeing your child's actions through the lens of their development and pausing to respond to their needs intentionally versus impulsively.' Through a depth of wisdom, insight, and practical examples, the authors show how this universal truth can be accessible to all of us. I only wish that I'd had this book when I was raising my children."

—**Gail Silver, JD, RCYT, E-RYT**, award-winning author of *Anh's Anger* and other books for children, and founder of The School Mindfulness Project Inc. and Yoga Child Inc.

"Practical, heartfelt, and clear, this book is an indispensable guide to parenting with wisdom and sensitivity. In this delightful book, Rachael and Helen weave together personal stories, accessible science, and down-to-earth tips for how to understand, connect with, and support your child's development. What a gift to our world!"

—**Oren Jay Sofer**, author of *Say What You Mean*

"Feel what a child feels, see what they see, and your day-to-day interactions might just be happier. *The Emotionally Intelligent Child* is a refreshing, well-written, evidence-based book that adds much to the world of *mindful* parenting. If you are interested in reducing stress and rekindling the oft-elusive magic of being a mom or dad, this book is for you!"

—**Kathy Hirsh-Pasek, PhD**, professor of psychology at Temple University, senior fellow at the Brookings Institution, and coauthor of *Becoming Brilliant* and *Einstein Never Used Flashcards*

"This book slowed me down and made me notice how I'm engaging my own kids and others, too. As parents and educators, we think continuously about the things we're doing, saying, and playing around our kids—or, more honestly, the things we're *not* doing, saying, or playing. Rachael and Helen offer reassurance, explain plainly how kids view and experience their world, and offer helpful ideas for any grown-up to parent with more confidence and caring."

—**Gregg Behr**, coauthor of *When You Wonder, You're Learning*

# THE EMOTIONALLY INTELLIGENT CHiLD

## Effective Strategies for Parenting Self-Aware, Cooperative & Well-Balanced Kids

RACHAEL KATZ, MS, ED
HELEN SHWE HADANI, PHD

New Harbinger Publications, Inc.

## Publisher's Note

NEW HARBINGER PUBLICATIONS is a registered trademark of New Harbinger Publications, Inc.

New Harbinger Publications is an employee-owned company.

Distributed in Canada by Raincoast Books

Cover design by Sara Christian

Acquired by Ryan Buresh

Edited by Cindy Nixon

### Library of Congress Cataloging-in-Publication Data

Names: Katz, Rachael, author. | Hadani, Helen Shwe, author.
Title: The emotionally intelligent child : effective strategies for parenting self-aware, cooperative, and well-balanced kids / Rachael Katz and Helen Shwe Hadani.
Description: Oakland, CA : New Harbinger Publications, [2022]
Identifiers: LCCN 2021059016 | ISBN 9781684038152 (trade paperback)
Subjects: LCSH: Emotions in children. | Emotional intelligence. | Parenting. | Child rearing.
Classification: LCC BF723.E6 K37 2022 | DDC 155.4/124--dc23/eng/20211208
LC record available at https://lccn.loc.gov/2021059016

Printed in the United States of America

24   23   22

10   9   8   7   6   5   4   3   2   1          First Printing

# Contents

# An Introduction to Your Child's Mind

Angela's mom, Rene, wiped her eyes and blew her nose. "I just want Angela to be happy. She feels sad at preschool and says other girls won't play with her. When I tell her to find someone else to play with, she snaps at me and says I'm dumb. I just don't know what to do." Rene's mind was spinning with the same thought: her 4-year-old daughter was lonely and didn't have any friends. And that was hard to hear.

Sean looked at his phone; it was 4:43 a.m. "Just go back to sleep," he mumbled to himself, but his mind was replaying his son Asher's behavior at Thomas's birthday party that day. Asher (3 years old) pushed Thomas over, in front of all the guests, when Thomas gave him a yellow cupcake instead of a blue one. What made Asher do this? Sean panicked at the thouwght of raising a spoiled child and wondered if he needed to be more strict with Asher.

Geoffrey was frustrated by Matthew's slow-moving actions. "Margot, he's just like you and your family. You're all a bit dreamy," Geoffrey said to his wife. "I wish Matthew would respond faster—he takes forever to do things." Geoffrey worried that children wouldn't have the patience to play with his 6-year-old son.

Chances are these stories sound familiar to you. You are not alone. They are familiar to most parents because a common desire for most parents, world over, is that their child will grow up to be a good person— that they will be kind, loving, and caring toward themselves and others. This requires guiding your child to become socially and emotionally aware of their thoughts, words, and actions, which takes time and effort.

To help build a child's social and emotional awareness, parents need to understand: (1) how and when children begin to think about mental states, such as thoughts, feelings, beliefs, and desires; and (2) how to explicitly talk to children about their behavior when they are young, while the seeds of social and emotional awareness are being sown.

Helen and I (Rachael) understand your parenting concerns. We are parents and professionals in the field of early childhood, the years from birth to 8, with decades of experience working with young children and their families. Helen is a developmental researcher with expertise in early childhood and creativity development, and I am an early childhood educator with years of experience as a teacher, administrator, and content creator for children's media and educational products.

Helen and I met at the Discovery School, the on-site preschool of the Bay Area Discovery Museum (BADM), where I worked as the head of school and Helen directed BADM's research team at the Center for Childhood Creativity. We spent many hours together discussing child development and applying this knowledge to practical teaching approaches. After observing and recording children's behaviors, we noticed that they became more self-aware, controlled their impulses better, and used perspective-taking skills more successfully when they were explicitly encouraged to consider the nature of their own and others' mental lives. When we intentionally supported the children's *theory of mind* (ToM)—a developmental continuum along which a child cultivates the ability to think about mental states—the children came to understand, consider, and respect that people have beliefs, desires, and intentions that often differ from their own.

We applied our knowledge of ToM and related research on child development to inform our classroom practices and to build the children's social-emotional skills. We wanted our students to become familiar with their mental lives—for example, to understand self-awareness and how to self-regulate and at the same time consider the mental lives of others. We wanted our students to think about their actions in relation to others, be helpful and cooperative, and demonstrate compassion.

Helen and I knew the skills that provide a strong foundation for success in school and beyond, and we knew the science on how children learn. We were able to apply and share these skills with the families and children we worked with at BADM and wanted to share this knowledge with a wider audience—with parents like you.

Parents are often left in the dark about their child's social and emotional learning—in particular, ToM development, which is a well-researched topic in academic circles, but not often discussed in applied settings. Our idea was to move this research beyond the labs and early childhood development journals to parents and caregivers. You deserve to know about this research because knowing more about the development of social and emotional learning can help shape your child's early social skills and mindsets. Our intention is to provide an accessible summary of meaningful research on the developmental continuum of social and emotional intelligence and offer an applied framework to help your child as they develop.

## Reading About Parenting vs. the Experience of Parenting

There is a balance among parenting, reading about parenting, and putting what you read into practice. Many of the parents we've worked with say they don't have the time to slow down, to play with their child, or to read about parenting. When they do slow down, they are met with the wonder of child development and sometimes the fear that they are parenting the wrong way.

Fran, the mother of a preschool student, referred to what she did as "automatic parenting." Her weekday mornings, for example, followed the same routine. She got out of bed, headed to the kitchen, and turned on the coffeemaker before heading to her children's rooms. She checked her younger child's diaper, reminded her elder to use the toilet, helped both children get dressed and brush their teeth, then headed back to the kitchen to get breakfast ready and make lunches. Fran responded swiftly and quickly when things deviated from the norm.

There were days, however, when Fran slowed down to observe her children and tried to imagine what they were experiencing from their perspective. When she did this, she noticed more. She wondered about her children's motivations and carved out time to read books and blogs on parenting and child development, but she was unsure how to apply what she learned to her parenting routine. She did her best to follow the tips and advice she read. Sometimes the instructions worked out well, but more often than not, they didn't. She wondered what she was doing wrong. This doubt weighed heavily on how she viewed her parenting skills, so then she'd avoid reading about parenting and return to her usual ways. After some time, the cycle would start again when something took her out of automatic parenting mode. She would stop to take the perspective of her kids, find delight in what they were doing, read about their development, and get confused again. Fran isn't the only parent we've met trapped in this cycle.

## Why This Book Is Different from Other Parenting Books

It is common to seek out a parenting book when you are unsure about something. There may be a conflict between you and your child, you may be looking to improve your parenting, you may believe something is not right with your child's development, or all of the above. Many books promise a quick fix to your concerns. They promise transformations if you follow a series of simple steps. These books imply that there is a right way to parent, and if you don't follow these steps with your child, then you are not raising your child correctly. What many of these books forget to mention, however, is that each child develops in their own way, in their own time, and perceives experiences individually. The same holds true for parents.

There simply isn't a quick and easy fix to parenting. You will not be a perfect parent, nor will you have a perfect child. Honestly, we don't want you to strive for this because you will miss out on the beauty of human development. We are always learning, developing, growing, and changing—this is core to our humanity. A huge part of our development, beginning at birth, is reading the emotional cues of others to determine how to connect with one another. Social and emotional intelligence lies at the foundation of our development, and we refine these skills as we age.

This book presents an approach to parenting that we call the "MIND framework." It is designed to help you develop a deeper awareness of your parenting and to see the world as your child perceives it at different stages of their development. Using the MIND framework, you will learn to see your child growing and changing socially and emotionally, at every moment. We want you to notice these changes, celebrate them, and know how to facilitate and enhance your child's social and emotional development.

## Overview of Reading Journey

Raising a socially and emotionally intelligent child involves seeing your child's actions through the lens of their development and pausing to respond to their needs intentionally versus impulsively. In doing so, you will be modeling social and emotional intelligence to your child. Throughout this book, we ask you to have conversations with your child about their mental life, specifically talking with them about their inner world while it's developing. These conversations help your child understand that everyone has a mental life that needs to be respected and that their actions impact themselves and others. This also helps plant the seeds of social and emotional intelligence—self-awareness, compassion, and self-regulation—early in their development.

Social-emotional skills, like many other skills, are malleable, and you play an important role in supporting your child's development of these skills. We believe that knowing the progression of ToM in relation to other key aspects of child development will help answer such questions as: (1) How are your child's actions impacting their relationships with others? (2) What might your child be telling themselves about the experience they are having? (3) What are they assuming about the point of view (beliefs or desires) of others? (4) How can you help shape their experience so that their inner voice remains kind and open-minded toward themselves and others?

The book is divided into two parts. Part one provides an overview of the development of social awareness and emotional balance by looking at the developmental progression of ToM, communication and language, and executive function skills, along with how each of these relate to your family culture and values. This discussion serves as a tool for you to use when considering the stages of human development while raising your child. We have included creative graphics to illustrate key developmental progressions and practical findings from social-cognitive research and to model techniques and instructions.

Part two introduces the MIND framework—an easy-to-follow guide to help you parent more patiently and proactively and to foster your child's emotional balance and social awareness. The MIND framework is a clear and practical guide that can be readily applied to measure and monitor your child's social and emotional development. You will use what you learned in part one and apply it to the MIND framework to step into the perspective of your child during their development of ToM and social cognition.

This book is intended as an actual framework for parents to adopt and employ, so we suggest that you refer to it often. Parenting can be an extremely busy and sometimes overwhelming endeavor, so pace yourself as you read the book and practice applying the framework to inform your parenting. We are here to guide you by sharing our experiences as researchers, educators, and parents who see the promise and power of developing strong social and emotional intelligence as the foundation of healthy development and learning.

# CHAPTER 1

# A Peek Inside Your Child's Mind

Have you ever gone from happy to frustrated in a matter of seconds? Sometimes our minds are trapped in the past—ruminating on reactions—and at other times our minds are projecting into the future, anticipating events and their outcomes. Mental states can affect how we feel about ourselves and our interactions with others because we observe them in the mind. This observational ability helps us consider our mental states, such as emotions, thoughts, intentions, desires, and beliefs. We witness how these mental states impact our relationships with others. As humans, we can observe how something like rumination becomes judgment, shame, blame, speech, and behavior. But we are not born with the ability to do this; it takes time and development to understand our mental states. Let's contrast your ability to do this with your child's.

## A Parent's Mind

Prior to becoming a parent, your mind was already busy navigating your mental states—swirls of thoughts, feelings, beliefs, desires, aversions, and more. Most of what was on your mind was centered on you, your relationships, and your experiences. Maybe after a long and stressful day at work, you spent time thinking about your current job, wondering if you should look for something that offered a greater sense of purpose. Or perhaps during a dinner conversation, as your partner spouted their opinion about your favorite movie, you doubted if, in fact, this was the right relationship for you. Essentially, your attention was devoted to you.

Once you became a parent, a fundamental mind shift happened that suddenly caught you off guard. Now you not only have to navigate the mind of another human being in addition to your own, but you also play a critical role in shaping your child's mind. There is no manual on how to navigate your mind *and* your child's. Although books such as this one will help, you and your child are unique, and it takes fine-tuning your thoughts, emotions, and beliefs in order to incorporate outside advice to meet and support your parenting goals.

Parenting can be overwhelming. It's not uncommon to find yourself preoccupied and distracted by thoughts about caregiving and your child. These thoughts are invasive. *My child took two bites of lunch today—will they ever grow with so little nutrition? Why are all the kids in the baby group walking except for mine? Is my child's physical development delayed? I sounded just like my mom today, and I promised myself that I would be different. What's wrong with me?*

Parenting is a mind-occupying job. If you were asked right now what is occupying your mind, what would you say? Turn inward for a moment. Can you identify your current thoughts and feelings about your parenting? Just notice them. As an adult, you have the ability to be aware of your thoughts and feelings (which is sometimes easier said than done). You are also probably curious about what your child is thinking and feeling because you understand that their thoughts and feelings are often different from yours. But your understanding of the mind is very different from your child's because your child needs time to develop an understanding of the mind and the ability to be self-observing.

# A Child's Mind

Children are energetic, enthusiastic, and curious, and they show strong emotional reactions and preferences from a young age that may leave you wondering what's on their mind. If you stopped to ask your toddler or preschooler to pause and share their thoughts, beliefs, and intentions, however, they may look at you quizzically (and then probably go back to what they were doing). Instead of answering you, they might ask a question about something they see in the kitchen or make their favorite stuffed animal dance on the table. Your child is not holding back from sharing their beliefs and intentions with you. They may behave this way because, developmentally, their understanding of the mind is not yet set, so they are unable to observe their own thoughts and feelings to then share with you.

Children are still developing a theory about what the mind is. As you might imagine, the evolving ability to comprehend mental states, both your own and those of others, is a complex process. Children go through many phases in their understanding of the mind that are closely linked to their development of language and other skills, including self-control, memory, and flexible thinking (also known as "executive function," which we will discuss more in chapter 3).

Before reacting to your child for dancing their stuffy on the table instead of answering your questions, pause and consider whether your child's behavior was *intentional* (a planned, calculated response) or *developmental* (an age-based response). By seeing behavior in this way, your responses will be less reactive and more thoughtful and compassionate.

Without knowledge of how the mind develops (and the other developmental continuums that support it), you might feel like Darin's dad, Ira. He was deeply concerned that Darin would not be able to make friends because of his son's volatility. Darin had very little emotional control at home. Everything caused him to become angry or upset. Ira believed that Darin's inability to see the impact of his behavior (which

Darin was too young to understand) would lead to struggles in school and in life. Projecting the fallout of his son's developmental behavior far into the future made Ira sad and angry, resulting in a subtle aggression toward his son. Ira admitted that he had a hard time seeing Darin's positive actions and believed that Darin was just being manipulative when he behaved well. If only Ira knew more about social-cognitive development and how he could talk to Darin about the impact of his actions, he could have a different approach to helping his son.

Guiding your child's development requires an endless amount of patience and kindness, especially toward yourself. But it also requires knowledge about how children develop to understand what shapes their thoughts, behaviors, and actions. A lot of the shame you feel as a parent could be alleviated if you understood whether your child's social and emotional behavior is intentional or developmental. Having more knowledge about how and when children develop an understanding of such mental states as thoughts and feelings will help you better parent your child.

Additionally, to give you an insider's perspective on how your child learns about social interactions from their peers, we will share with you, in this chapter and throughout the book, what we have witnessed children do and say in school and learning environments outside of the home, such as children's museums and after-school classes. You may often wonder where your child learns expressions and actions that are not said and done at home and are not aligned with what you're modeling. Your child is constantly learning from others. Although you may at times want your child to focus on learning from you, providing opportunities for your child to experience the point of view of others—in particular, their peers—helps them develop social awareness and emotional control. They would have no need to be socially aware and to hold back their emotions if everyone felt the same way they did.

# Your Child's Developing Theory of Mind

It's easy to notice when infants and young children start to crawl, walk, say their first words, and ask questions. In other words, milestones in children's physical and language development are often relatively clear to spot. This is not always the case, however, with some aspects of social-cognitive development, which are far from transparent and change at a rapid pace, especially during the early years. This may leave you questioning things like:

- How do you know when your child understands that another person might not like their favorite food (that is, when other people have other desires)?

- How do you know when your child starts to understand that people might be feeling one way (for instance, sad) but express a different emotion (say, happiness)?

- How and when does your child begin to think about their thinking and the thinking of others?

In order to be emotionally intelligent and socially aware, we all need to think about our thinking and to take the perspective of others. So questions like these are the focus of theory of mind research—an area of study that investigates individuals' understanding of their own and others' mental states, including thoughts, emotions, beliefs, desires, and intentions.[1] One very broad way to watch ToM in action is to notice that young children tend to have a hard time thinking about the perspective of others because, developmentally, they are not yet able to do this. For example, it is hard for young children to believe that other people may *not* like eating animal crackers. To your child, they are the most delicious snack in the world. They cannot fathom that not everyone feels this way.

# THEORY OF MIND

## FROM BABIES TO SCHOOL-AGE KIDS

### BABIES

Your baby is responsive to others' emotional expressions and can learn about the world from social interactions.

*Eleven-month-old Layla waves and shouts "hi" to every person she sees. She notices their eye contact, waves, and smiles, and so continues to repeat her efforts to greet others.*

### TODDLERS

Your toddler begins to notice that different people have different desires and the resulting actions and emotions that emerge when those desires are either fulfilled or not.

*Alex, 22 months old, eats his lunch of macaroni and cheese with delight. He watches closely, however, as his twin brother Karl, bursts into tears and dumps his plate on the floor.*

### PRESCHOOLER
### younger

Your young preschooler can understand that people act according to their beliefs and that others' beliefs might differ from theirs.

*Three-year-old Kate ran to hide behind her mother whenever she saw a dog, as she believed all dogs to be scary creatures. Her friend Sebastian thought dogs were friendly and tried to pet the dogs he encountered.*

Figure 1

# THEORY OF MIND

## FROM BABIES TO SCHOOL-AGE KIDS, *continued*

### PRESCHOOLER
**older**

Your older preschooler grasps that people might have false beliefs about the world (i.e., someone's belief differs from reality).

*Dad will be so surprised!*

*Eli, 5 years old, helped his family prepare a surprise party for his dad's birthday. Eli knew his dad thought (falsely) that it would be just an ordinary day.*

### SCHOOL-AGE
**younger**

Your school-age child adds another layer to their understanding of mental states when they realize that people can hide their feelings from others.

*"Let's trick Papa!"* whispered 6-year-old Monica to her mother. *"We'll tell him that we didn't have any fun today at the beach."* She tries to look disappointed when she tells her father they had a terrible time.

### SCHOOL-AGE
**older**

Your older school-age child can recognize that even if it appears that someone is not thinking, the mind is always at work.

*Seven-year-old Kai sat concentrating with his pencil just touching the paper but not moving.* "I'm thinking about all of the stories I could write," *he told his dad when he came to check whether he had finished his homework.* "My mind just won't stop thinking!"

Figure 1

Another way to gain a better understanding of ToM is by looking at how psychologists measure it in children. Researchers have conducted a multitude of studies investigating how children come to understand that people can have different mental states.[2,3,4,5] Many of these studies examine when children pass a *false-belief task*.[6] What is a false belief? Sometimes what we believe differs from reality. For example, Melanie thinks that her favorite mint tea is in the cupboard, but in reality, it is in a container on the kitchen counter (because her husband moved it without telling her). Her behavior—where she will look for the tea—is driven by what she believes. So she will act on her false belief: she will look in the cupboard for the tea because that is where she thinks it is. The ability to attribute a false belief to others is considered a key milestone in the development of ToM, and children typically understand false beliefs around age 4 to 5.

Seeing false belief from a child's view might look something like this. Jeremy and Bruce were looking for a container to hold the caterpillar they found in the yard. Jeremy remembered there was an almost-empty box of Swedish fish on his kitchen table. The boys could eat the candy and then use the empty box as the caterpillar's new home.

When Jeremy's sister, Talia, came home, she saw the box in the yard. From a distance, Jeremy and Bruce saw Talia open the box. Before they could warn her what was inside, she screamed, hurled the contents, and started to cry. Angered and embarrassed by the incident, she chased Jeremy and Bruce, saying they tricked her. She threatened to tell on them if they didn't turn over the candy. Talia had a false belief about what was in the box, similar to Melanie's false belief about the location of her mint tea. But she reacted differently, with anger and embarrassment (and justifiably wanting the candy she was looking for). Children—and some adults—often react unpredictably to their false beliefs until they are able to recognize, developmentally and cognitively, that what they inferred is not true.

Psychologists sometimes measure ToM in children with what's called the "Sally-Anne test," one of the most well-known and frequently used false-belief tasks.[7] In this task, children are shown two dolls named Sally and Anne and told the following story:

*Sally has a basket, and Anne has a box. Sally puts a marble in her basket and then leaves the room. When Sally is away, Anne takes the marble from the basket and hides it in the box. Sally then returns to the room.*

Children are then asked where Sally will look for the marble. If children understand false belief, they will say that Sally will look in the basket because that's where she *thinks* the marble is. Most studies find that 3-year-olds typically say that Sally will look in the box (where the marble is in reality), but 4-year-olds tend to get the idea that Sally will look in the basket. The Sally-Anne test cleverly taps into children's understanding that others may have different levels of knowledge, which drives other people's behavior.

It is useful to picture your child's ToM development as a continuum to understand the progression of how children learn to sense what others think, believe, want, and intend. Understanding this progression will help you age-appropriately nurture your child's social and emotional development, as well as help frame your expectations about your child's behavior and your parenting.

This developmental progression leaves you with a lot to consider. For instance, knowing your toddler doesn't fully understand that there is diversity in people's thoughts could explain why your child hit their friend when they did not share a toy truck. That is, your child has not yet developed the ability to consider whether their friend would be willing to hand over the truck just because your child wanted to play with it. Additionally, the conflict-resolution approaches you suggest on sharing might be too complicated for your toddler to grasp because, developmentally, your child is still learning that others think differently than they do.

Now that you have a basic understanding of what ToM is, how psychologists measure it, and some of the major milestones in ToM development, it's valuable to take an in-depth look at some of the research that shows the progression from infancy to later childhood. Understanding how and when some of the key ToM concepts develop will boost your parenting confidence and help you see your child differently. Wearing this scientific lens will help ease your reactions to your child, allow for some mental space between you and your child (which is not to say that you love your child any less), and build confidence in your parenting.

# Theory of Mind in Infants

It may be surprising to you that researchers have found convincing evidence that infants display behaviors that are important precursors to ToM development. Think of this research as "pre–theory of mind," similar to how prekindergarten prepares your child for school. So what is your infant doing that will contribute to their emotional intelligence and social development?

## Your Infant Is Studying Your Face

Infants crave social interaction and are easily upset if they feel disconnected.[8] The classic "still-face experiment" clearly shows this. Infants sit in their car seats facing their mother or father. The infant naturally coos, smiles, and gurgles when they see their smiling parent. The parent is then instructed to turn away for a brief moment and turn back and look at their infant with a blank expression. The infant tries to engage with the parent by smiling and cooing again, but this time, there is no response. The interaction quickly goes downhill, and the baby often gets very upset. What this tells us is that, from a very early age, babies are quite responsive to the emotions and the social interaction they get from the world around them.

Here's how the still-face experiment relates to everyday scenarios. Think about the countless times that you put your child in the car seat. How often are you engaging with your child as you do this? Your child is watching the expression on your face, carefully. As they study you, they respond to the emotions and interactions they observe. If your child gets fussy, take a moment to check where your mind was at the moment. Were you thinking about dinner? Or were you frustrated by the buckle on the car seat, wishing you had spent those few extra dollars to buy the better brand? Notice where your mind went, come back to the present moment, and determine which face you would like to offer your child to make a positive emotional connection.

## Your Infant Begins to Understand Intentions

A critical feature of social-cognitive development is understanding that others' actions are driven by intentions.[9] When your child spills milk all over the table, for example, you will most likely react differently depending on whether that action was intentional or not. Were they upset because they didn't get juice instead of milk, or did they accidentally tip over the cup? A clever and often-cited study by developmental psychologist Andrew Meltzoff suggests that before their second birthday, infants are starting to understand the intentions of others.[10] Meltzoff showed 18-month-olds an adult trying to complete a target action—for instance, pushing a button with a stick—but the adult failed to complete the action. Then infants were given the chance to perform the action. Even though the infants never saw the completed action, many of them produced the intended action (that is, used a stick to push a button). But there's a twist to the study. In a second experiment, infants witnessed a robot do the same action as the adult (fail to push the button with a stick). But in this case, the infants tended not to produce the target action. These findings strongly suggest that infants appreciate that desires drive behavior and at some level understand a fundamental aspect of ToM: that people, but not inanimate objects, have goals and intentions.

When you play with your child, that play often involves toys or objects—things that you can both focus on and interact with. Think about your actions and what you are saying to your child when the two of you are playing with blocks, for example. Imagine that you and your child sit down to build a train shed for their toy trains. Your child has tried three times to build the roof, but the blocks keep falling down, so they stop building to watch what you will do. As your child is collecting new information about the physical world (how you stack the blocks to make the roof), they are also learning about your goals and desires (your shed looks different than what they were trying to construct—it is much wider). Making your intentions explicit by talking about them ("I am going to build the shed extra wide because I want three cars to fit inside") can help your child assess your intentions and gradually learn to predict the effects of their actions and those of others.

## Theory of Mind in Toddlers and Preschoolers

Watching your child grow from an infant to a toddler is a big transition for you and your child. You probably rejoiced when your child started walking so you didn't have to carry them anymore. But that excitement may have been short-lived when your child started getting into everything and childproofing became your second profession. Another big milestone in this period is children's ability to use words to communicate what they are thinking and feeling and, of course, what they want. If your child is speaking, do you recall their first words? How did you feel when your child spoke to you for the first time? We've met many parents who remember tears welling up in their eyes when they were first called "Mama" or "Dada."

In addition to the big steps (literally) that children make as they enter toddlerhood, they make huge strides in their ability to understand mental states. Research has revealed some important emerging understandings of desires and emotions in the years leading up to preschool, when children are just starting to talk, expressing their thoughts and emotions verbally.

For many children, much of their social and emotional development, including ToM development, happens in classroom settings—spaces in which parents and primary caregivers are not with their children. In these learning spaces, children explore and act on their thoughts, desires, and beliefs, and the responses they receive shape their social and emotional awareness. Interacting with other children provides a chance to explore how their worldview, including what they learn at home, differs from that of their peers. While young children are learning about their mind and the minds of others, they struggle with expressing their thoughts, desires, and emotions with one another. This can often lead to conflict and tears.

## Perspective Taking: Seeing into the Minds of Others

How often have you heard your child say "It's mine!" when encouraging them to share with others? When picking up her toddler from preschool, Beatrice was horrified to learn from her teacher that her daughter, Sarah, had an aversion to sharing. When playing on the playground, Sarah had grabbed the ball from Abigail and pulled it close to her, then threw a handful of dirt at Abigail and screamed when Abigail tried to take the ball back. Horrified, Beatrice scooped up Sarah, apologized to the teacher, and scolded Sarah on the way out. The other mothers began to whisper. Beatrice felt awful. On the drive home, her mind was full of questions. What was wrong with Sarah? Why wouldn't she share at school when she shared at home? Who was teaching her this selfish behavior? Maybe she should change schools. Beatrice Googled "child psychologists who help with sharing," wondering whether Sarah needed some professional help. Have you done this too? If so, you are not alone.

Many parents are confused and frustrated by their child's inability to share with others. Why do young children have such a hard time sharing? One reason is that sharing involves the ability to take another's perspective. Little did Beatrice know that most of the toddlers at school believed the ball belonged to them.

# YUCK OR YUM
## THE BROCCOLI-GOLDFISH STUDY

Researchers Repacholi and Gopnik (1997) used the fact that almost all children prefer goldfish crackers over broccoli to demonstrate that starting around 18 months, children can recognize that someone else has a different desire.

Experimenter shows the child that she DISLIKES GOLDFISH CRACKERS but LIKES BROCCOLI

(the opposite of what most kids like).

"EWWW, yuck!"    "Mmm, yum!"

Then experimenter asks child, "Can you give me some?"

## RESULTS

The 14-mos-olds will give the experimenter what the CHILD LIKES

(goldfish crackers)

The 18-mos-olds will give the experimenter what the ADULT LIKES

(broccoli)

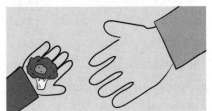

Figure 2

When do young children develop perspective-taking skills? A prolific area of developmental research has examined children's appreciation of others' differing mental states, such as desires. A University of California at Berkeley study, for example, demonstrated that children as young as 18 months appreciate that others have desires that differ from their own.[11] When an adult experimenter expressed her dislike for Goldfish crackers and her love of broccoli (which was opposite to the child participants), 18-month-olds appropriately gave that adult broccoli when she asked the child to "give me some." Notably, children just 4 months younger tended to give the adult Goldfish even when the adult clearly expressed that she did not like to eat them. That is, 14-month-olds did not recognize the perspective of the adult and gave the adult their own preference, the Goldfish crackers.

Understanding and taking into consideration the perspective of others is a skill that continues to be challenging throughout life. Think about the last time you had a disagreement with your spouse, coworker, or friend. Chances are that one reason for the problem was not taking the time to understand the other person's perspective. Similarly, parents often find themselves at odds with their children when they do not consider their children's thoughts, desires, and intentions. It is human nature to want others to accept our perspective rather than appreciating the perspective of another person. The ability to view a situation from different perspectives forms the core of emotional intelligence because it helps us make sense of others' thoughts, feelings, and actions.

## Observation Informs Children's Beliefs

Remember the studies about how infants attend to social cues? As your child studies you, they are trying to make sense (with the limited knowledge, skills, and experience they have) of your intentions and beliefs. *Why does Dad keep putting peas on my plate when he knows I don't like them?* Your child may not understand the intention behind people's actions, so they are not yet able to think, *I know my nutrition is important to Dad, so he's going to keep serving me peas, thinking I'll eat them because they're good for me.*

Understanding another's intentions, beliefs, and desires prepares us for how to respond socially to them. Your child's understanding of mental states helps them respond socially to others. For example, if your child sees that another person is upset or hurt, they may offer a favorite toy or blanket to comfort them. During the toddler and preschool years, your child spends copious hours observing others, responding with words and actions to test out what they are learning from their observations. This is why we see children doing the same things over and over, and when the results stay consistent, your child forms a belief about what they observed.

Adults often explain and predict human behavior in terms of mental states.[12] Psychologists refer to this as a *belief-desire framework*. If you are hungry for ice cream, you may walk to the corner market to buy some. Your behavior can be explained by *assuming* that you *want* ice cream and *believe* that the store down the street sells ice cream. One widely held theory regarding the belief-desire framework is that children start with an understanding of desires—often referred to as a *simple desire psychology*. In a seminal series of studies, Henry Wellman and Jacqueline Woolley found that children as young as 2 years of age first construe human action in terms of desires.[13]

In these studies, 2-year-olds were told stories about a character who wanted to find something. For example, children were told that Johnny wanted to find his dog and that his dog might be in the house or in the garage. Then they watched as a cardboard cutout of Johnny walked to one of the locations and found either his dog or something else. The children were asked to make judgments about the actions and emotional reactions of the story characters. If Johnny did not find his dog in the first place he looked, children were asked if he would look in the second location or stop searching. With respect to emotions, children were asked if Johnny would be happy or sad if he found (or did not find) his dog. Overall, 2-year-olds were able to predict the actions and emotional responses of the characters. In other words, these findings indicate that young children's early understanding of human action can be characterized as a simple desire psychology.

Children often use desire psychology in the classroom. Toddlers greet each other differently than older children do. Instead of saying good morning, they bring over their friend's favorite toy, showing simple desire psychology in action. That is, children understand that bringing over the toy that their friend desires will lead to their friend feeling happy. The friend usually notices the gesture and smiles when receiving the favorite toy, thus building bonds of understanding.

## The Art of Deception

You, like most adults, understand that thoughts and beliefs have the power to comfort or harm others. Your toddler or preschooler is just laying the foundation for this understanding. Because children learn through doing to broaden their understanding, you might witness a lot of behavior that appears to be mean, which can be deeply upsetting to you. When you watch your young child behave unkindly toward another child, you immediately feel like a bad parent. Remember, much of what you are witnessing is your child learning about intentions, desires, and beliefs and the natural consequences that follow this understanding, like deception.

A study investigating children's understanding of desires asked the young subjects to deceive a puppet to get something they wanted (a desirable sticker).[14] In what's known as the "Mean Monkey study," children were shown a few different stickers and asked which one they really wanted. Then they were introduced to the Mean Monkey puppet. The children were told that Mean Monkey would always choose the sticker they wanted most. After this, the children were asked to point out their favorite sticker. The key strategic element in this game is for children to deceive Mean Monkey about the sticker they really want so the monkey will choose another one. Even after many trials of the same game, 3-year-olds fail to lie and are left with a pile of unwanted stickers. In contrast, 4-year-olds tend to get the hang of the game and successfully deceive Mean Monkey.

This study is helpful to remember when you begin to notice your child telling lies. It goes without saying that your goal is to raise an honest child, but lying reflects an important landmark in ToM development. Lying (and deception) requires an understanding that other people have different beliefs and that those beliefs may not reflect reality. Young children regularly test out the power of deception, with some of them understanding and developing the skill before others. They test out their understanding on their peers, especially those who pick up the concept later. The children being fooled are unable to challenge the deceiver because they don't understand the concept yet. It's easy for adults to spot deception in young children because most young children don't understand that their actions are visible to others.

Here's an illustration of this involving two of my preschool students. For several months, I witnessed Tom deceive Chester at school. It was only a matter of time until their parents came to me with their concerns. Tom's mom was upset that he was lying, and Chester's mom was furious that Tom upset her son. I explained that they were witnessing the development of understanding that others have beliefs and desires that might differ from their own and how this leads children to test out the concept of deception. It was a painful process for both parents.

Tom would watch Chester, observing his likes and dislikes, and then test out his observations by fooling him. Tom noticed that Chester loved playing with the red truck, so Tom devised a myriad of ways to keep the red truck from Chester and then noted how Chester would respond. Deceiving Chester became a fun game. Once, Tom told Chester, "The teacher gave the red truck away this morning. She said it was broken." Chester wailed, and Tom stood watching, confirming his understanding of the important link between his actions and how they impacted another's emotions. Tom had an extensive vocabulary and was quite talkative and observant. In contrast, Chester was quite shy and could play alone for long periods of time. Tom was not intentionally trying to hurt Chester, but he liked seeing how Chester would respond to his lies, learning that words have the power to deceive.

To a child, this is a pretty cool discovery. Rest assured that the string of lies you will hear your child tell during these years is common. Most young children do not want to cause harm, but sometimes they are unaware of the relationship among their thoughts, actions, and emotions.

Talking to your child about their inner world and pointing out how their thoughts differ from those of others is very important. Teaching children about ToM while they are laying the foundation for understanding their own and others' states of mind enriches a child's awareness. You are reinforcing the concept that we all have different thoughts, beliefs, and intentions that guide our actions and that our assumptions about the minds of others have the power to comfort or harm them. The best way to help children comprehend lying and deception is to explicitly discuss them. Let your child know when you recognize that they are trying to deceive you (or someone else). Then model and talk about perspective-taking skills from the view of the deceiver and the deceived. My conversation with Tom about Chester and the red truck went something like this:

"Good morning, Tom," I said. "When you came to school this morning, I saw you take the red truck and hide it behind the puzzles, and when Chester arrived, you told him that I took the truck away." Tom looked at me. His eyes seemed to ask, *How did you know?* and he was surprised to learn that I was observing him. Tom looked confused, so I explicitly told him that I was watching him to reinforce the understanding that people are individuals who see each other and that we question the actions of other people. I asked, "What did Chester do when you told him I took the truck? How do you think he felt when he heard the news?" Tom just continued to look at me.

I used paper and crayons as an aid to our conversation. When you want to talk with your child about their inner world, a great way to encourage them to share is to draw while talking. Using pictures to illustrate thoughts and feelings helps them stay focused and shows how to reflect. (Don't worry about the quality of the drawings; you don't need to be an artist—stick figures will do!) We talked about Tom's thinking and how to deceive someone. When he said something, I drew a speech bubble over him, and when he talked about his thinking, I drew a thought bubble. I explained the difference between them. Tom shared his thoughts and I drew pictures of them, so the paper became a screen from his mind. Tom paid attention, retaining the conversation by looking at the pictures. We talked about how words and actions can deceive someone.

Next, I drew Chester and asked Tom to think about his friend's thoughts and feelings. As soon as Tom saw this relationship on paper and talked about it, he changed his behavior toward Chester. He would grab the truck and hand it to Chester. In turn, Chester relaxed more while he was playing and often passed the truck to share it with Tom. In the end, Tom and Chester became quite good friends. The red truck reappeared in the classroom, and the boys understood that although they have the capacity to deceive others, honesty is a better choice than deception. In fact, Tom became an advocate for truth, reminding his classmates not to lie.

Like Tom's and Chester's parents learned to do, you can apply these techniques to talk about your child's thinking and the harm of deception. It can ease your judgment. For example, Chester's parents no longer saw Tom as mean, and Tom's parents immediately wanted to help Chester. They continued to talk with Tom about deception with the drawing technique. You, too, can shift your own perspective while your young child is learning about perspective taking.

# Theory of Mind in School-Age Children

As your child matures, so does their understanding of ToM. Generally, when children reach around 6 to 8 years of age, they begin to develop an understanding of *interpretive theory of mind* (IToM), or comprehension that individuals can have different ideas about the same situation.[15]

## Recognizing Diversity of Thought

One simple way to conceptualize IToM is to think about optical illusions (like the classic bunny versus duck image). While some people see a bunny when they look at the image, other people see a duck, and these are both reasonable interpretations of the picture. This ability to recognize diversity (as well as commonality) in people's thoughts is an important social-cognitive skill that emerges in middle childhood and continues to advance across the life span.[16]

## Awareness of Stream-of-Consciousness Thinking

Another interesting aspect of mental state understanding is recognizing that even when a person is not really doing anything in particular, their mind is still at work in a stream of consciousness. John Flavell, considered by many to be the grandfather of ToM research, investigated this concept in 3- to 8-year-old children and young adults.[17] In front of the participants, two experimenters first explained that when one of them was asleep, her mind was empty (and showed an empty thought bubble), but that when she was on her way to school, her mind was full of thoughts (and showed a thought bubble with asterisks, or "ideas," in it). The participants were then asked to indicate whether an experimenter would be thinking or not while sitting waiting, looking at a picture, and solving a problem. The researchers found that, in general, preschool-age children did not yet fully understand the concept of a stream of consciousness (that the mind is constantly full of thoughts and ideas); however, with increased age, individuals demonstrated greater knowledge that even when someone is waiting or sitting idle, their mind is still at work.

It takes a long time for your child to fully grasp the idea that everyone they meet will have thoughts that may be similar to or different from theirs. And until they do, they are simply not aware that we all have minds full of thoughts that can be hidden from others by our actions.

Now when your 8-year-old argues with you about sleeping at their best friend's house on Saturday night, despite having been home from school for three days at the beginning of the week with a fever, think about their development. Think about it when the conversation becomes hot and heated and you hear, "Mom, you have your idea and I have mine. Why do I always have to listen to your idea?" As you feel your shoulders tighten and your lips purse, pause before reacting to look beyond the argument. Consider the incredible journey of ToM development your child is on, how it started, and where they are now.

In this chapter, we've talked about children's understanding of the mind, that it starts in infancy and continues to expand throughout life. Start to notice how your infant responds to your smiling (or frowning) face. This is their way of engaging with you socially before they can communicate with you using words. As your child starts walking and talking, they are paying close attention to people's goal-directed behaviors and intentions. Also around this time (as your child approaches their second birthday), your child starts to appreciate that other people may like different things ("I like jelly beans, but Mom likes chocolate"), which is the foundation of perspective taking and the core of emotional intelligence.

Their perspective-taking skills continue to develop in the preschool years as they consider how people's beliefs may differ and drive their (and other people's) actions. A key milestone in ToM development happens in the later preschool years, when children understand false beliefs—when we act according to what we believe is true (looking in the pantry for cookies), even if that differs from reality (your daughter ate all the cookies last night). As your child makes the important transition to school, their ToM continues to develop as they start to appreciate that people can have different thoughts and beliefs about the same situation and that mental activity does not have an on-off switch; instead, our minds are in a constant stream-of-consciousness state.

Your child's ToM development happens within the context of many other areas of growth, including language. Thoughts can't develop without language, and language can't develop without experience and interaction. In the next chapter, we explore how to promote your child's communication and language skills to support their social awareness and emotional balance.

# PART ONE

# Encourage Your Child's Core Development

Now that you have a sense of the continuum of theory of mind development, you can start watching how your child is learning about their thoughts, feelings, beliefs, and desires in relation to others. These developmental changes occur as they learn to take the perspective of others. Your child's ToM development does not happen in isolation, however, as they are simultaneously strengthening other cognitive domains, such as language development and executive function, as well as being influenced by culture and compassion—all of which supports their social and emotional growth. Let's step further into their developing mind so you know how to, age appropriately, bolster their emotional intelligence.

# CHAPTER 2

# Use Language to Shape Social Awareness

Siera, 3 years old, loved to use the word "distracting" without understanding what it meant, and she tried it out in many different contexts. One afternoon, she raced around the playground wanting to be caught. "Come on, distract me!" she yelled to her mom. Learning language can be both a playful and a frustrating experience, as I learned when I moved to China several decades ago and felt like a child learning to talk.

Like Siera, I spent many hours a day using words in the wrong context. I didn't know how to ask for the shower rings that hold the curtain to the rod, so for two months, my bathroom was covered in water—the sink, floor, and countertops were wet. I wished everything I needed was in my direct sight so I could just point and say "this," the way your child does when they don't know the word for what they want. Sadly, the rings were nowhere to be found; with a limited vocabulary, I tried to tell people what I wanted, but no one understood. Your child does this too.

Every failed attempt to explain what I needed made me angry. The shop attendants tried their best to understand me, but inevitably, I would leave the store empty-handed and irritated. My cold, wet bathroom with the shower curtain balled up in the corner became synonymous with my inability to communicate my needs. Without the spoken language skills, it was hard to make myself understood. Imagine the frustration a young child feels.

To me, the Chinese language was just random sounds, similar to how language might sound to an infant—a barrage of spoken gobbledy-gook that seemed to make sense to everyone but me. I was exhausted from the focus required to listen and the effort it took to make myself understood. It's the same for your child: they are processing and inte-grating language all day every day.

Communication with language keeps us connected; it is the bridge between self and other. Therefore, it plays an essential role in shaping social and emotional intelligence. Children learn to communicate from their nuclear and extended family, friends, caregivers, and even strang-ers, but the role you play during the early years makes an impact through the questions you ask, your tone of voice, and your body language. Your child is paying close attention to the language you choose, how you interact with others, and how your words match what you do. You model positive communication in ways that matter.

Language is a complex system of units (words) that can be assem-bled into an infinite number of combinations (sentences). Amazingly, your child learns the underlying structure of language and how to use it to communicate with relative ease and often with much excitement (think about your child's joyful babbling or their endless stream of "why?" questions).

About nine months after I arrived in Beijing, the sounds started to make sense. I was in the locker room at the gym when I began to rec-ognize nouns and verbs—"socks," " shorts," "to run." In that instant, everything changed. I was no longer an observer of my world, but a participant. I could comprehend words and say them out loud. Think of how the world changed for your child when they started to talk.

Most children start uttering their first words around their first birthday and are speaking full sentences and asking questions by the time they are 3 years old. It does take patience, understanding, time, and love to guide your child's communication and language skills. But like Siera, the child on the playground, and me in China, your child will use language that they learn from others and say things they don't understand. As you help your child with their vocabulary, you will see how they learn to refine what to say and how to say it. The stories and research in this chapter will help you understand how your child learns to speak and communicate, and you will gain methods for effectively guiding them to develop the communication skills that contribute to emotional and social awareness.

## The Sounds of a Language

Your child begins from infancy to learn the language that is spoken at home and in their community. What babies hear and how they learn language has been a focus of developmental psychology and linguistics research for years. Although researchers have made great strides in understanding how young children acquire a language (and sometimes two or three at the same time), psychologists, neuroscientists, and linguists have yet to solve the perplexing puzzle of how young children learn a language so quickly and easily.

To begin with, your child needs to master the sounds that are used to make their spoken language. The world's languages consist of about six hundred consonants and two hundred vowels, but each language uses only about forty *phonemes*, or speech sounds.[18] How do infants know which sounds are part of their native language? Research by psychologist Patricia Kuhl and colleagues shows that babies are born "citizens of the world," meaning they can discriminate all of the sounds of all of the languages around the world.[19] But by around 10 months, babies turn into "culture-bound listeners" who are only able to distinguish between sounds in their native language (similar to adults). Kuhl and her team tested American and Japanese infants on distinguishing the sounds "ra" and "la" (sounds that are important in English but not in Japanese).[20] At 6 to 8 months, babies from both countries could distinguish the sounds. But two months later, the babies in the United States were getting a lot better at telling the difference between "ra" and "la" while the babies in Japan were getting worse. Kuhl's research indicates that babies lose the ability to discriminate sounds of all languages before their first birthday.

In a matter of months, infants begin to produce the sounds they hear. Soon the sounds transform into words and sentences, and before you know it, your child is speaking. When you think about it, listening is the key to language. Try listening as deeply as an infant does, without regard to the actual words; imagine you are listening to a foreign language that you can't understand. Pay attention to every detail to try to deduce the meaning of the words. Where is the speaker looking? What hand gestures or body language are they using? What does the speaker's tone of voice, pace, or intonation communicate? What is the speaker's facial expression? Notice how much you can figure out without knowing the meaning of the words when you focus completely on how people of all ages express their needs and desires.

As you listen to and observe your child's early language skills, reflect on the following questions:

- Which sounds have they mastered? Which sounds are they practicing now?

- Is your child demonstrating curiosity about language? How do you know?

- In what other ways does your child communicate with you?

- What happens when you don't understand what your child is attempting to tell you?

A common source of frustration for preverbal children is their inability to communicate. Remain calm and approach the situation as a puzzle for you to solve. Encourage your child to show you what they need by pointing to it or moving toward it. Follow their gaze to try to decipher their message and provide lots of language as you do so: "Do you want the green cup or the purple bowl?"

# The Language Explosion Begins

You may have noticed that your child started responding to your requests ("Can you put the block in the bucket?") well before they started talking. This demonstrates the difference between *receptive language*—understanding the words and expressions of others—and *expressive language*, which is using words and phrases to express your thoughts. As mentioned previously, most children start talking at around 12 months, but research shows that starting at around 6 to 9 months, infants can understand that words are associated with objects.[21] So although your baby may not respond with words when you ask "Where's the apple?" they understand some of what you are saying—that "apple" refers to the red, round object in front of them—and they can use that knowledge to continue to build their language skills.

If babies don't start talking until around their first birthday, how do researchers investigate how children start learning language? You won't get much from asking infants, "Can you tell the difference between those two sounds?" Researchers need to be really creative in designing experiments to get into a baby's head so we can deduce what they do and do not understand. One way for babies to tell us what they are thinking—or, more specifically, whether they notice a difference between something they just heard and a new stream of sounds—is by looking toward new sounds. Infants, like adults, get bored of listening to the same thing and tend to "perk up" and pay attention when they hear something new.

This can guide your interactions. When your child continues to drop food on the floor no matter how many times you tell them not to, stop asking the same way. Try changing your tone of voice or replace a noun or verb with a new one so your child pays more attention to what you're asking. For example, "Stop dropping food on the floor" becomes "Kernels of sweet corn go in your mouth. Chew, chew, chew … one for me, one for you." Not only is this fun for your child to hear, but they also learn words in a new context, tune in to repetition, and hear rhyme—all ways to play with language. When you use words in different contexts—the orange pumpkin on their shirt and the orange slices they ate for lunch—that helps your child learn that words can have different meanings and functions. And while repeating words may get boring, research finds that parents who repeat words more often to their infants have toddlers with stronger language skills.[22] Lastly, rhyming is both enjoyable to listen to and it helps your child learn how sounds form words. As described in chapter 1, infants around 18 months old start to understand and interpret the intentions of other people.[23] That is, they pay attention to the social contexts in which words are used. This research demonstrates infants' ability to use the relationship between eye gaze and labeling to learn the name for a new object at around the time that many children are going through a "vocabulary spurt" or "naming explosion." Sometime around 18 months, most children experience a sudden growth in their spoken vocabulary and are learning approximately ten to twenty new words each week.[24]

The learning process can look something like this: At 15 months, Roxanne was constantly chattering, and even though she'd acquired only a few words that could be clearly distinguished, she would use them to learn more about her environment. When she wanted to touch something, she would look directly at it, point, and say, "More!" If her mom didn't immediately give her the object to hold, Roxanne would look back to ensure that her mother was paying attention. Then she would return her gaze to the object and continue pointing and saying "MORE!" louder and louder. Once the object was in her grasp, she would hold it and ask "Dis?" and wait for her mother to tell her the name of the object.

Dare Baldwin conducted a study that showed that 18-month-olds use an adult's focus of attention as a cue to word meaning.[25] In this study, infants were shown two novel objects that were placed in two separate buckets. The experimenter then peeked into one of the buckets and said, "There's a *blicket* in here." The adult then gave the child both of the objects. When asked for the "blicket," the children tended to pick the object that the adult had been looking at when saying the label. Your child is learning from how you label things as you relate with objects, even before they are able to speak.

This research highlights that you should talk to your preverbal child even when you don't think they are listening because, in many cases, they are paying attention and understanding much of what you say. Label things you see ("I see a blue bird with big wings"), narrate what you are doing as you make dinner ("Now we put the pasta in the pot"), sing to them when they are taking a bath. Take every opportunity to talk with and to your child because they understand much more than you may think—and remember to use your words wisely.

# Effective Ways to Build Emotional Vocabulary

There are multiple approaches you can take to support your child's growing vocabulary, particularly their language in the areas of social and emotional awareness. Here are some recommendations.

## Talk with Your Child About Feelings

Once the naming explosion begins, so has the next phase of connecting with your child. Your child has been and will continue to build language skills through direct experience—touching, tasting, watching, and listening to the world around them—and they will listen as you label and describe what they are exploring. You can help expand their vocabulary and develop social awareness and emotional intelligence by talking about emotions in many different settings. For instance, when you're at the playground, take advantage of another child's melt-down to discuss emotions while your own child is calm.

One afternoon while eating a snack at the playground, 3-year-old Peter witnessed a child on the swings crying and screaming for his mom to come push him. When Peter's dad noticed that Peter was closely watching this other child, he used it as an opportunity to talk with Peter about feelings. He began by describing what they were both seeing and hearing: "That child is crying and screaming, kicking his legs, and flailing his arms." He then asked Peter to practice identifying emotions. "How do you think that child is feeling?" When Peter was quickly able to say "sad," Peter's dad followed up with, "Why do you think he's feeling sad?" Peter was so confident with his responses that his dad ventured further to help him transfer what he was watching into his own life: "Can you think of a different way the boy could tell his mom what he needs? What would you do if you had to wait for me to push you on the swings?" Peter thought hard until he came up with an idea. "I know! He could do this!" Peter put his snack down, went over to the swing, put his belly over the swing, and ran with his legs back and forth to swing by himself.

Research supports the actions of Peter's father, finding that talking to children about emotions is one of the main predictors of *emotional competence*—how children learn to express and control their emotions and recognize emotions in others.[26] Practice labeling emotions you encounter throughout your day, whether in a book or movie character, yourself, or another child on the playground. In addition to identifying the emotion, it is important to discuss *how* you identified the emotion: "It seems like you're mad because your face is scrunched up, your shoulders are tight, and you're shaking your fist at me."

Understandably, good feelings like happiness and gratitude are easier to talk about than negative feelings like sadness or anger; however, talking about negative feelings is equally vital. It helps your child under-stand what causes negative emotions and, importantly, how to express them.[27] When your child throws a tantrum at the supermarket, the last thing you want to do is talk about why they are feeling the way they're feeling, but taking time later (when they are calm, after you get home or even the next day) to talk about what they were feeling in that moment can help your child process those feelings and better recognize them in future experiences. It is also helpful to discuss ways to deal with challenging emotions, like pointing out how the character in a book needed some quiet time by herself to calm down after getting upset. During these conversations, try not to do all the talking yourself—give your child lots of opportunities to suggest ideas and ask questions. In chapter 8, we will share more strategies to talk with your child about their emotional reactions.

## Balance Talking with Quiet Time

Although talking with your child about what they are doing is extremely beneficial, try to find the right balance between saying out loud what your child is doing and remaining quiet. Children also need time to explore and observe the cause and effect of their actions without being spoken to so they can process and integrate how to use words to describe their actions on their own. Silence can provide time and space for very young children to take initiative, demonstrate their interest and curiosity, or give them an opportunity to try something new. Self-directed quiet time allows your child to play without you (or another adult) saying, "Let's do this next." This kind of quiet time provides opportunities for your child to express their creativity and imagination and develop decision-making and problem-solving skills—all important components of developing awareness and control of their emotions.

Sam's parents, Meg and Austin, fought over this balance. Meg was quiet by nature, so she didn't talk much to 18-month-old Sam. She loved being with him and responded to him with smiles and laughs as well as the appropriate sternness. Austin was the opposite. He was chatty, could strike up conversations with anybody, and loved narrating

Sam's every move. Meg found Austin's reactions to be stifling, and Austin believed that Meg was stunting Sam's language development by not talking to him enough. It took time and understanding for Austin and Meg to eventually respect their style differences and the importance of finding a balance when interacting with Sam. Austin practiced listening to and observing Sam more, and Meg tried to boost Sam's vocabulary by reading more to him. In this way, she wasn't forcing herself to respond out loud to Sam. Through books, Meg was intentional about introducing Sam to language that he wasn't used to hearing in everyday interactions (words like "delicate," "joyful," "grateful," and "curious").

## Choose Stories That Build Emotional Vocabulary

Research with preschoolers suggests that eliciting talk about emotions when reading books with children can promote helping behaviors, like bringing a blanket to someone who's cold.[28] Talking about feelings and emotions when reading to your child can help build their emotional vocabulary and heighten empathetic helping tendencies. Reading to your child enhances their growing vocabulary and introduces the language of feelings and emotions. To build emotional vocabulary, look for stories that show relationships and use words to describe how characters feel. Even if the story doesn't specifically mention feelings and emotions, you can ask your child questions about the characters. Talk about how the characters feel, compare the characters' world to your child's world, and use illustrations to show how facial expressions reflect feelings and emotions. For instance, if a character's lunch was stolen, you might ask your child, "How do you think they are feeling now?" or "What would you say to the character to make them feel better?" Invite them to imagine themselves as a character in the story by asking, "How do you think you would feel if that happened to you? What would you choose to do in that situation?" Monitor your child's comprehension and share how you connect to the story. Tell your child how it made you feel and why. You can do this even before your child is talking or if they have a limited vocabulary because your child learns language by listening to what they hear.

You can also prompt your child to identify how someone is feeling by looking at their body language (like a furrowed brow and a down-turned mouth to express frustration). When viewing people on TV or on a phone with your child, ask questions like, "What is that person feeling?" "How can you tell?" and "What is it that you see in their face or body that makes you think so?"

Storybooks also introduce the power of narrative and how to share ourselves with others. By listening to stories, children discover how to use words in ways that bind ideas and thoughts together. They also learn to evaluate, infer, and reason—skills required for clear communication and emotional perception. Consider how most schools or child care settings read books to groups of children much the same way that you read a book to your child at bedtime. In a group, the conversations about stories often get the children to share their personal experiences and histories. They discover what they have in common.

I read the story of Hansel and Gretel to my class. Joseph (4 years old) eagerly shared with the class that he was like Hansel and Gretel when he got lost in the shoe store and thought his mother left him there. "I cried so hard and I got all hot! Then my mom saw me." Emma (4 years old) was particularly taken by his experience: "I get hot too when I cry!" She wondered how similar Joseph's experience was to Hansel and Gretel's: "Did a witch offer you cookies and candy?" Joseph quickly responded, "No, I wouldn't take the witch's cookie. I'd fight her off." Emma smiled. "You are brave, Joseph." Joseph agreed, "Yes!" The other children agreed with Emma's inference that Joseph was brave, and her comment opened the door to a discussion on bravery. We explored what makes someone brave. Was it possible to be brave but still feel scared? After our talk, the children's pretend play revolved around brave acts. Little did I know that Emma, Joseph, and the story of Hansel and Gretel would lead to this.

Even if your child is not talking yet, reading to them helps build important brain connections and a strong foundation for language development. As mentioned previously, children understand language well before they can talk. If your child is talking, they will likely ask to hear their favorite story over and over. Though you may get tired of reading the same story, know that your child is working hard to master the words from the pages, studying the social interactions of the characters, and using the pictures to put language into context. Repetition may not be so fun for you as a parent, but it is appropriate and beneficial for your child's language development. The more words your child knows, understands, and masters, the easier it will be to express themselves.

The toddler and preschool years are an ideal time to intentionally build your child's emotional vocabulary by talking, reading, and playing with them. Consider these reflection questions as you interact with your child in different scenarios:

- In what ways have you already built your child's emotional vocabulary (reading books, discussing movies, playing games)? What are a few new ways to try?

- Does your child understand that tone of voice, body language, gestures, and words all impact communication? If not, try sneaking in some practice with a game to build their understanding. Say the same words using different tones of voice, body language, and gestures, asking your child to identify what you were actually communicating and distinguishing that from the words you said. Try something simple like "No way!" to express surprise, rejection, and disbelief.

- What are you communicating to your child with your tone of voice, body language, gestures, and words? Think of a recent situation in which your child felt unsure about something. Did your demeanor, in addition to your words, communicate your message to your child?

# Play Develops Emotional Language Skills

Another great way to boost your child's language, including emotional language, is through play. Even though it might seem like a waste of time to play when you have to get dinner on the table, finish yesterday's laundry, or check off another task on your to-do list, remember that play is how your child learns. According to esteemed child psychologist Jean Piaget, "Play is the answer to how anything new comes about."[29] And play provides the ideal context for children to develop emotional language and communication skills.

Your child likely spends hours engaging in pretend play by turning boxes into spaceships, organizing tea parties for their stuffed animals, and transforming your living room into a grocery store. The act of pretending has captured the attention of many researchers because make-believe play is a particularly striking feature of young children's play. When your child engages in pretend play with peers, they are planning which roles they and their peers will take on, exerting self-control to keep in character, and often flexibly adapting to adjust their role as the story evolves. In fact, research supports that children who engage in more pretend play tend to be more advanced in language, memory, and reasoning[30,31] and also tend to have a more sophisticated understanding of other people's thoughts and beliefs.[32] A unique feature of pretend play is that it offers your child an opportunity to practice emotion regulation, which ranges from your infant self-soothing by sucking on their hand to your preschooler or grade school child becoming more conscious of emotions and developing strategies to manage them (taking deep breaths, counting to calm down). By pretending to be another person and acting out how they perceive a situation during pretend play, your child can better take on the perspectives and emotions of others and regulate these feelings. So take part in your child's pretend play.

The important role of adults in children's play is most evident in *guided play*, where adults support children's learning by carefully choosing props or materials or providing prompts during the play (often referred to as *scaffolding*) while allowing children to maintain control over their learning.[33] With guided play, you have a learning goal or intention (such as learning to distinguish a mad face from a sad face) and provide support while letting your child remain in charge. In guided play:

- Let your child control the situation while you intentionally add new language to the experience and model for them how to remain emotionally attuned when interacting with others.

- Watch, note, and then intentionally build vocabulary to help your child express their feelings. Think about the words needed to help build emotional vocabulary and then respond using key phrases that comment on and describe the emotion your child is exploring. Children appreciate and respond to language that is slightly advanced for them.

- Make a point of pausing to see how your child responds to you and to watch how they handle your emotions. Stopping, observing, and waiting for your child's response offers a glimpse into how they react to the emotions of others.

When my daughter was young, she loved dramatic play, so joining her pretend games in which she made the rules was how I helped build her emotional vocabulary. Many evenings and weekend mornings were spent in the pretend kitchen. Nina, my daughter (3 years old at the time), served me breakfast (no matter the time of day). "Here is your oatmeal and strawberries," she'd say while handing me a bowl filled with marbles.

The Emotionally Intelligent Child

One day, I planned to model disappointment and the language used to express it. My choice of topic was not random. Over the past few weeks, I had watched Nina struggle with how to express her disappointment. I pretended that I was disappointed with my oatmeal by communicating my feelings with language that was one level higher than Nina's. I told her, "I didn't want strawberries in my oatmeal. You didn't ask me, you just put them in. I'm so disappointed you didn't ask. I wish you'd asked me if I wanted berries. When the berries touch the oatmeal, they change the flavor of the milk." I repeatedly used the word "disappointment," which was new to Nina. She knew and used the words "sad" and "angry" in her vocabulary, but not "disappointment." I waited for her response.

She looked at me, and I could tell she was thinking about what I'd said. "Oh," she quizzically replied.

I went on. "Yeah, I'm just so disappointed. I was hoping that my oatmeal would have brown sugar on top and the strawberries would be on the side."

Nina looked at me again, then picked up the bowl of marbles. "I can help, Mommy," she said, and then placed her hand on my cheek.

"Oh, Nina, your hand on my cheek makes me feel less disappointed," I replied with a smile.

For Nina, a new emotion had been registered. In this short exchange, the seeds of understanding disappointment had been planted. And now Nina and I could build on the concept.

To build your child's emotional vocabulary, intentionally label emotions you are modeling and inquire about your child's emotion. Once the new emotion has been introduced:

- Expand on it by sharing the belief or desires that sparked the feeling

- Describe the physical sensation from the feeling ("Disappointment makes me feel hot and prickly")

- Rephrase your child's response and explain how their response made you feel

Communicating with your child in this manner enhances their emotional vocabulary and models self-awareness by connecting how thoughts, beliefs, and desires manifest in actions, feelings, and emotions. Given that the interaction is pretend, your child will feel safe and secure practicing regulating their emotions with your guidance.

## More Than Just Words: Using Language in Social Contexts

While you are busy building your child's emotional vocabulary, remember that language and communication are more than just words. Children need guidance to effectively communicate with others. The key to helping your child learn to communicate is paying attention to what is said, what is *not* said, and how it is said, along with offering tools to help your child say what they mean.

The use of language in social contexts is referred to as *pragmatics*. Pragmatics includes skills like initiating conversations, keeping on topic in a conversation, using appropriate body language and intonation, and providing the appropriate amount of information when someone asks a question. For example, if someone asks, "Do you have the time?" it would be considered rude (and weird) to answer, "Yes." In many cases, pragmatic ability requires understanding a speaker's communicative intention. For example, saying, "That looks delicious" can mean different things depending on how it's said. Indirect speech ("Could you pass the milk?") and metaphors ("life is like a roller coaster") are other examples of pragmatics. With respect to language, children use a variety of pragmatic cues to help them learn to communicate. These are skills your child builds over time.

# Social Referencing: Reading the Emotions of Others

When your child looks at you for reassurance, they are engaging in what psychologists call *social referencing*. They use your facial expression to decide how to deal with a novel situation. Infants and young children often rely on their caregivers' facial expressions and tone of voice to regulate their response toward people and new situations. Think about the following situation: Ruby, a really curious 1-year-old, is playing in the yard when the family cat, Dusty, walks up to her. Ruby reaches to grab Dusty's tail (and yank it with all her might) when she turns toward her mother and sees a stern look on her face. Ruby is not very likely to pull Dusty's tail, fortunately, because she looked to her mother for clues on whether it is safe to grab Dusty's tail.

Researchers have studied social referencing in babies who are just starting to crawl by using the "visual cliff," a large plexiglass-topped table with a checkered pattern.[34] In the middle of the table is a visual drop-off (what looks like a sudden drop, but the surface is actually uninterrupted and completely safe to crawl across). The baby is placed on one side of the table while the mother stands on the other side with a fun toy. The mother is instructed to smile or make a fearful face. In most cases, when babies see a smiling face, they crawl across the cliff, but if they see a fearful face, they choose not to cross the visual cliff. Infants start to use social referencing before their first birthday, but older children (and adults) also use it to read ambiguous situations.

Think about a time when your child looked to you for reassurance in a new or potentially scary situation, like approaching a dog at the park, visiting an unfamiliar place, or walking into a classroom at a new school. A simple smile (or frown) can often be more effective than words in communication with your child. Consider one of my students, Kim, and her experience starting at a new school, where she was not fluent in English like her teacher and peers. The story illustrates the importance of social referencing and the power of nonverbal communication.

When Kim was 5 years old, she moved from Korea to attend an international school in China, where the common language was English. Her mom, Saeri, was concerned that Kim would have no friends because Kim's English was very limited. How could Kim communicate with her teacher and friends without speaking English? Saeri did some reading on language development and learned that at Kim's age, she would understand the concept of body language—hers and others'. She told Kim that to help her communicate with her new teacher and friends, she could learn from other people's actions and tone of voice. That even though she could not speak English, she could understand what her classmates and teacher were feeling by watching what they do. Similarly, Saeri advised her daughter to also pay attention to her own actions because others could tell how she was feeling from them. Saeri suggested that Kim seek out classmates who looked happy and at ease because they might be more open to playing with her even though she couldn't talk with them. Finally, she told Kim that if her body language was gentle and inviting, the children might be drawn to her.

On the first day of school, when Saeri left the classroom, Kim stood motionless in the doorway. Then she turned back to look at her mom. The sweet, confident smile on Saeri's face said, *I believe in you. You're going to be fine.* And Kim was fine. In fact, she was more than fine. Over the next several weeks, Kim did what her mother suggested and carefully observed her peers. She studied their movements, actions, and exchanges. She watched the other children with a calm curiosity, an attunement that matched a Zen master. Kim paid attention to her own body language and facial gestures, which had a neutral quality to them. Even though the children could not speak with Kim, they were drawn to her—maybe because they did not feel judged.

Gina, a child in Kim's class, ran hot and cold and used actions to make her peers uneasy. In the morning, she would be Suzanne's best friend, and by the afternoon, Gina would disinvite Suzanne to her party. The inconsistent behavior was very confusing to the other children in the class. Kim spent time watching how Gina and the other girls interacted. With Kim's limited English, she timidly told me, "Gina pretend kind." Kim noticed that Gina's body language did not match her words. I asked Kim if she would share with the others how to read body language. She taught all her classmates the importance of body language.

One day after school when Kim's mom came to pick her up, I told her that Kim taught the class about body language, which she was delighted to hear! Saeri told me that she taught Kim about body language by first explaining to her the developmental progression of how she learned language and then how to enhance a skill set (in this case, body language). Saeri reminded me of the importance of explicitly teaching children, ages 5 and older, about their development and that they can watch and enhance their own development. The reason Saeri's technique worked so well is because kids love learning about how they used to be and what to expect in the future.

A fun way to teach your child about body language is by playing catch with a ball. First, describe body language to your child by explaining that you can show your feelings and convey emotions and ideas through your posture, movements, and facial expressions. Let them know that you can express ideas and feelings without speaking and that others can figure out what we want to say from how we act. Then explain to your child that a conversation is similar to passing a ball from one person to the next—the ball represents words. We pass words back and forth to each other. When unkind comments are passed to us, we tend to pass them back.

Ask your child to pay attention to the tone of your voice and your physical gestures when you pass the ball. Frown, cock your head, squint your eyes, and say, "It's so much fun to play with you!" Ask your child whether what you said matched the way it was said. Your face and body said you weren't having fun, but your words said something different.

Now ask your child to have a try. Ask them to respond to what you said by passing the ball back to you and remind them that the ball represents the back-and-forth of a conversation. How did they respond? Were they "pretend kind" like Gina? How did it feel to receive this message? How can you match your tone, body language, and what is said?

Playing this game will encourage your child to notice how speech, tone of voice, and body language need to align in order for a message to be received properly. Keep playing this game until your child secures a deep understanding of the impact of body language. Assess their understanding of this concept by letting your child take the lead in passing the ball. Can you guess what feeling they are trying to convey? Do their actions, body language, and tone all say the same thing?

## Language and Theory of Mind Overlap

In chapter 1, you learned about your child's theory of mind, or mental state understanding. When ToM and language overlap, your child experiences some incredible development. Thinking requires language. Imagine the overlap in this way: As your child develops, they use their language and communication skills to express their thoughts and ideas not only to others, but to themselves as well. It is much easier to reflect on a past experience, identify intentions and needs, and understand yourself and others when you have a large vocabulary and clear communication style.

By 3 years old, your child makes connections about why things happen. They are busy making connections between the cause and effect of things (for example, when they blow on their birthday candles, the flame goes out). They rely on their language skills to give explanations and make connections among desires, emotions, actions, and outcomes. Your child's thinking and logic might have a few gaps, but imagine your child's sense of pride and consider the tremendous development they have undergone to be able to share their thoughts and speculations with you.

By around 5 years old, your child's development takes another giant leap. Using language and thinking, they recognize that they can reexperience an emotion from a memory. In the same way that you can become angry when you think about a past disagreement you had with your sister, your child can now do the same. They can feel frustrated with their best friend when they remember that, yesterday, the friend said their LEGO sky fighter wasn't that powerful.

Also around the time when your child is transitioning from preschool to kindergarten, they learn that emotions can be hidden from others—that a person can feel one way on the inside but not show it on the outside. When Henry turned 5, his mother told me that he suddenly became very quiet. He used to talk out loud (sometimes too loud) and share what he was thinking and doing. She recalled that he would make up stories with his trains and talk about where they were going, who they were taking from place to place, and what happened when they broke down. Now she had no idea what was going on in his head. She was concerned about why he'd stopped talking and also why, at times, he appeared visibly angry. After talking at length with Henry, we discovered that he was struggling with thoughts and wasn't sure what to do with them. On a regular basis, he was telling himself that he was stupid, especially when his first attempt to complete a task was unsuccessful. Now that he'd learned he could hide his feelings, he was choosing to stay quiet.

Henry's shift from being a chatterbox to more pensive and quiet was a normal developmental shift that I explained to Henry's mom in a conversation about the overlap of language and ToM development. Henry was now at an age that he could think about his thinking, and his inner thoughts could affect his moods and the perception of his experiences. I shared with Henry's mom the technique I learned from Kim's mom: to explicitly teach your child about the developmental phase they are in, model it, and offer suggestions for how to enhance it in a fun and playful way.

Henry's mother shared with him that now that he was able to think about his thinking, he could have conversations with himself using an inner voice. Then she explained that he had a choice to believe what he was telling himself. She suggested listening to what he told himself and asking whether it was true, assuring him that he didn't have to believe his inner voice. Henry listened with curiosity. Next, Henry's mom shared a personal story with him about her own inner voice. Children love to learn that their parents have struggles similar to their own. She told him that sometimes her inner voice tells her she's a bad scientist at work and that when she believes what she tells herself, she gets sad and mad, then quiet. Henry was so relieved to hear that his mom did the same thing. They discussed how silly it was that they tell themselves that they are not smart. Henry reasoned that it was not a good idea to be mean to themselves; his mom smiled and agreed. They were both discovering self-compassion from the conversation.

It is important to talk with your child about their development, especially when important shifts happen, like Henry discovering his inner voice. Most of the time, we let children experience development, but we don't explicitly talk with them about the changes. Think of it like this: your child is learning about language and communication, and then they suddenly discover that they can use language to speak only to themselves—that words can stay in their mind without being said out loud and that they can use body language to hide what they are thinking and feeling.

Brendan, 6 years old, tested out this new phase of development by constantly trying to trick his parents. He told his parents that he had brushed his teeth when he had not and that he didn't go on a field trip at school when he did. Brendan's father was particularly irked by this behavior and wanted to punish him for lying. In fact, Brendan was attempting to use the power of language to disclose certain information to his father to see whether he could fool his dad. Brendan's dad talked with him about this stage of development, and together they brainstormed appropriate (and inappropriate) contexts in which to withhold information. This is a powerful discovery—for children to learn that what they're experiencing, and testing out, is part of human development and that there is a time and place to play with language.

As you observe how your child's language and ToM develop in tandem, reflect on these questions:

- What aspect of language is your child currently developing? How might you share and discuss this concept with your child?

- Is your child's inner dialogue active? How do you know?

- What are some ways you might consider connecting with your child to better understand what they are thinking and feeling, especially after they are able to hide their thoughts and feelings?

In this chapter, we've focused on connecting with others through language. Language is a powerful tool that enables us to bond with others and understand ourselves. Patience, understanding, time, and love are needed to guide your child's development of language and communication.

Talk to your child often and early; they are able to understand long before they are able to speak back to you. Talk to your child even when you don't think they are listening because, in many cases, they are paying attention to much of what you say. Play with language by singing, rhyming, and using gestures and body language to keep your infant and toddler engaged with language, and remember that your child relies on social referencing—using your facial expressions—to decide how to deal with a novel situation.

Your preschooler learns that language and communication are more than just words. Pragmatics—the rules that guide turn taking, body language, and how individuals interact with one another—become increasingly important as your child engages with peers and adults in different environments. They need guidance to effectively communicate with others. Provide opportunities for role-play in which your child has to explain the same thing to different people (their teacher or a friend), or play "emotion charades," having players act out different feelings as a way to teach body language. The key to helping your child learn to communicate is to pay attention to what is said, what is *not* said, and how it is said, along with offering tools to help your child say what they mean.

You can dissect the body language, tone of voice, eye contact, facial expressions, and gestures of characters when watching television or other families at the park. It is also helpful to reflect on your own interactions and conversations with your child and acknowledge your mistakes. Allowing your child to see when you miscommunicate and what steps you take to fix it helps them understand that it will always take work to communicate clearly. Now is the time to intentionally build your child's emotional vocabulary by talking, reading, and playing with them.

Children aged 5 and older enjoy learning about their development and how to amplify it. Talk with them about how they used to be and what to expect in the future. Explicitly talk with your child about their language development—how these skills will change as they age and how to improve them. Help your child understand that language and communication are used to express their thoughts and ideas to others, as well as to themselves through their inner voice. Remind them to pay attention to what their inner voice says and that they can choose to believe or reject what they say to themselves, especially when the comments are unkind and not useful.

As your child interacts with others, they are learning how to adapt their behavior in such social environments as school playgrounds and family events. Successfully navigating those situations often requires inhibiting certain behaviors, balancing emotions, and being able to self-regulate. In other words, your child is calling on their executive function skills to pause, make good choices, and select how they intend to work with others. In the next chapter, we explore the core components of executive function and how you can help your child build these skills to promote flexible thinking and reflection.

# CHAPTER 3

# Foster Flexibility and Reflection Through Executive Function

Mimi's voice-mail message sounded tense as she said, "Call me as soon as you can! I can't take it anymore. I'm bouncing off the walls watching Max bounce off them." Her tone was tinged with sadness, anger, and exhaustion. Max had energy, this was a given, but during the COVID-19 pandemic, when Max, like many children in the United States, had to attend school virtually, he was having a hard time attending kindergarten online. Mimi, his mom, watched as he jiggled, danced, and played with the computer keys while his teacher was talking. Mimi urged him to pay attention, questioning his inability to focus. "You're a big boy now, Max, you're in kindergarten. You need to listen to the teacher and do what he says. Just sit and pay attention, and when school is over, I'll take you for an ice cream." Max liked that idea, said he was sorry, and went back to school.

Five minutes later, he was wiggling again. Mimi became angrier and angrier until she screamed, "Just sit still! You're in school." Whether in virtual classes or a traditional school, it would not be entirely surprising to see Max struggle when told to sit still. Young children learn by actively doing things, having their senses engaged, and interacting with other children. In contrast, Mimi was assuming that it was easy for him to control his behavior.

Have you ever felt like Mimi, perplexed and frustrated by your child's actions? I remember when my son, Jacob (who was around 3 at the time), kicked over the sandcastle he built with his best friend (that they'd worked on for two hours) because it seemed like a "fun" thing to do. His friend cried inconsolably. Most days, I was like a broken record telling Jacob how to act and treat others. I'll bet you can relate.

It can take a while to move beyond your child's actions to think about what you are asking them to do. Before doubting your child and your parenting skills, it helps to understand, developmentally, what your child is able to do with respect to controlling their impulses and thinking about how their actions will impact others. When you do this, you are asking your child to utilize their *executive function* (EF) skills— a set of complex cognitive processes that allow us to monitor and control our behaviors and make informed decisions. But how developed are these skills at each age? Gauging this determines how you can effectively respond to, and guide, your child's behavior through cultivating flexibility and reflection.

## Executive Function in Social and Emotional Development

EF is a powerful predictor (in some cases, even better than IQ scores) of children's success in school and beyond.[35,36,37] EF has received increased attention from the popular press and academic researchers because components of EF are essential for school achievement and for behaviors that entail teamwork, leadership, and social awareness. EF helps us plan and prioritize tasks to balance workflow, think about the role that others will play to complete tasks, and set and achieve goals. We are required to use EF skills in almost everything we do—when learning, interacting with others, doing something time-bound, and more.

# EXECUTIVE FUNCTIONS

## COGNITIVE SKILLS THAT CONTROL BEHAVIORS

### INHIBITION OR SELF-CONTROL

helps your child make decisions by resisting impulses to do something that they would later regret. *Example: not pulling the cat's tail, even though it looks fluffy, to avoid getting scratched.*

### COGNITIVE FLEXIBILITY

is closely linked with creativity and problem solving, and allows your child to consider different perspectives and strategies. *Example: transforming your kitchen stool into a tree house for teddy bears.*

### WORKING MEMORY

allows your child to hold and mentally manipulate information in their minds. *Example: keeping track of the names of their Pokémon action figures.*

### FOCUS OR ATTENTION

is critical for achieving both short and long-term goals. *Example: tuning out the distractions of a buzzing light and a crying baby sister to focus on homework.*

Figure 3

The core components of EF include self-control, cognitive flexibility, and working memory. An additional component that is important for social-emotional development is focus or attention.[38] When we think about EF, we tend to think about it in relation to children's academic learning; however, we have come to see that this view is too narrow. In fact, research suggests an important link between EF skills and understanding emotions.[39] We see that young children are continually problem solving during social interactions. EF skills can be described in the following ways. Have you seen your child using these skills?

**Inhibition or self-control** helps your child make decisions—hopefully, smart ones—by resisting impulses to do something that they would later regret (like not pulling the cat's tail, even though it looks fluffy, to avoid getting scratched). In social settings, this requires your child to resist acting according to their first instinct because that action may impact someone else negatively. For example, imagine that 5-year-old Edward's 3-year-old sister picked his favorite red toy car out of the basket. Instead of grabbing the car out of her hand, he was able to negotiate a sharing plan with her. His mom noticed his patience and told him he should feel proud of how he responded. Edward beamed from the positive reinforcement, noting the value of self-control.

**Cognitive flexibility**—sometimes referred to as "thinking outside the box"—is closely linked with creativity and problem solving, and it allows your child to consider different perspectives and strategies (such as transforming your kitchen stool into a tree house for teddy bears). This requires adjusting to the demands of relationships, which, by nature, are constantly shifting. Jessica and Todd (both 2½ years old) were playing with a toy xylophone together. Jessica struck the keys with the mallet and then passed it to Todd so he could have a turn. Jessica waited for Todd to pass the mallet back, but he didn't; he would not share. Jessica's mom watched her daughter navigate the situation. First,

Jessica looked surprised. After a moment, she picked up a spoon from the play kitchen and used it in place of the mallet. She smiled at Todd, who smiled back. Jessica then traded the spoon for the mallet to give Todd a try. Jessica's mom was impressed by her daughter's thinking; she'd handled the social situation with creativity and a smile.

**Working memory** allows your child to hold and mentally manipulate information in their mind and make connections between seemingly unrelated things (like keeping track of the names of their Pokémon action figures). It can be used to remember instructions when working with others to complete a task. For instance, Daniel and Brian (both 6 years old) made a plan to build a bridge with blocks for their race cars. Pretending to be engineers, they sketched out their idea. Daniel divided the tasks between them, and the boys began building. After working for some time independently, Daniel went to see how Brian's part of the bridge was coming along. Much to Daniel's surprise, Brian was not following the plan and had started building a house with his blocks. Daniel was furious and yelled, "What are you doing? We had a plan to build a bridge!" Brian was too embarrassed to tell Daniel that he didn't remember all the steps needed to complete his part.

**Focus or attention** is critical for achieving both short- and long-term goals (such as tuning out the distractions of a buzzing light and a crying baby sister to focus on homework). This is essential to observe social interactions and anticipate how someone might respond. Maggie (5 years old) watched her grandma struggle to make school lunches for her brothers and sisters. Maggie asked how she could help. Her grandma was touched and relieved to have someone help her. Maggie's grandmother placed an extra cookie in her lunch.

The beloved children's television show *Sesame Street* dedicated an entire season to promoting EF—in particular, self-control—by featuring Cookie Monster and his insatiable love of cookies. Rather than just eating every cookie in sight, Cookie Monster had a new mantra: "Me want it, but me wait." Dr. Rosemarie Truglio, the program's senior vice president for curriculum and content, made the important point that the show targets preschool children, which is the best time to promote EF skills because they are primed to learn them at that stage of development.[40] Building your child's EF skills in the early years yields great payoffs down the road. And one of the best ways to start teaching your young child EF skills is to model them. Consider these questions as you think about how to support your child's growing EF skills:

- Think about a time when you were particularly taken aback by something your child did. Which EF component was dominant in what you observed?

- In figure 3, which aspect of EF seems most challenging for your child when interacting with others?

- In your own actions, which EF components are readily on display for your child to see?

- Is there a particular EF component that is more challenging for you to apply in social situations? Compare this with your child's tendencies, appreciating the strengths in both of you while acknowledging potential areas for improvement.

## What the Ability to Wait Reveals

Cookie Monster's struggle to wait and exhibit self-control highlights the key question of one of the most famous pieces of social science research—the "marshmallow test." Namely, given the choice between a small reward now or waiting for a bigger reward later, which would you choose? Stanford psychologist Walter Mischel investigated that question with preschoolers in the classic marshmallow test back in the 1970s.[41,42,43] In this assessment, children are typically presented with one tempting item (for example, a marshmallow) and told that if they wait without succumbing to temptation or needing to call the adult back, they will be given more. The adult then leaves the child alone for a short period of time (usually around fifteen minutes). During this waiting period, children are challenged with finding the self-control to inhibit their desire to take the appealing treat right then in order to gain additional rewards if they wait.

Intriguingly, researchers have documented positive associations between preschool-age children's ability to successfully delay gratification (wait without eating the marshmallow)—which is essential to self-control—and a host of good outcomes later in life, including academic success and social-emotional coping abilities.[44] In fact, in 2020, many parents recorded themselves conducting their own adaptations of this experiment and posting them to social media platforms. You, too, can see whether your child is capable of waiting!

# The Critical Network of Simultaneous Development

As your child's understanding of self-control, adaptability, working memory, and focus grows, it happens in tandem with the development of language, communication, and theory of mind. In chapter 1, you learned about ToM and how your child develops an understanding of mental states, including thoughts, beliefs, desires, and emotions. Then in chapter 2, you learned about the critical link between language and ToM—it would be hard to develop ToM (like taking the perspective of a friend) without the language skills to think about mental states. Now consider EF, or more specifically, working memory, for example. Each time you ask your child to control their behavior, to pause before reacting, you are asking them to bridge the development of EF, language and communication, and ToM. This is a complex task! It requires a lot of skill and development to pause and think about your actions. Here's what you're asking your child to do:

- First, control their impulse with EF. ("Don't hit your sister when she takes a cookie off your plate.")

- Next, take the perspective of the other person through ToM. ("She had one cookie and you had three.")

- Then, process this information and form a response that will meet their needs and the needs of others. ("How can you act with your sister's feelings in mind?")

- Finally, express their thoughts to others clearly using language and communication. ("If you want her cookie, please ask.")

As you can see, there's a lot going on within your child's developing brain. It takes time and guidance to know how to build your child's EF skills. But now you know what to look out for, so you can keep your observations about their behavior within the context of their development. It's helpful to think of self-control, for example, in the following ways:

- Starting in infancy, your child might suck on their finger as a self-soothing technique. The sucking action calms them down—a form of self-control to avoid crankiness.

- Your toddler can wait for short periods, which shows they have some self-control. But when their patience runs thin, don't be surprised if they snatch something from a friend. Patience and experience are limited at this age, and their level of EF reflects this.

- Compared to infants, preschoolers have the additional months of experience from interacting in the world and show considerable growth with impulse control, flexibility, and patience. You may notice your child's budding EF skills when they spontaneously whisper to you at the library, knowing from experience that this is a place where you speak softly so you don't disturb others.

- Your school-age child may access their EF skills to think about, plan, and engage harmoniously with others, but don't expect perfection. It takes time for skills and actions to become habits.

- Tantrums occur at all ages and reflect your child struggling to regulate their emotions.

Children, and many adults, find it challenging to consistently exhibit successful EF capabilities. For instance, consider the last time you reacted strongly to a comment that someone made and then wished you'd controlled yourself better. Mastery of EF skills is truly a lifelong learning process. But there is a lot you can do to help your child build the EF skills needed for social and emotional awareness, because research has shown that EF processes are muscles that can be strengthened.

## Planning and Reflecting with Your Child

Child development and education experts created a preschool curriculum called Tools of the Mind for children to grow EF muscles.[45] In Tools of the Mind classrooms, preschool children create "play plans" to promote self-regulation. Children start their school day by drawing or writing which activities they intend to do that day, intentionally thinking about how they will accomplish their vision. Planning with intention helps children think and act purposefully, and when plans are modified throughout the day, this encourages children to think flexibly and be adaptable. Researchers examining the impact of Tools of the Mind have found positive effects on self-control and attention skills, as well as improvements in reading, vocabulary, and mathematics.[46,47]

If planning and reflecting builds the muscles of EF, especially self-control and working memory, what's the best way to do this with your child? This was a question I repeatedly asked when my son was 4 years old. He was strong-minded with a fiery temper. Often, he had very clear ideas on how things should be done and little tolerance when an outcome was not as he expected. He would take out his anger on his toys, friends, and family. I lacked patience and would blow up when he blew up. At times, I wasn't sure which one of us had a larger problem with impulse control. I hoped that my own self-control and working memory muscles would advance as I worked to build up his.

At the time, I used a planning template in my classroom that was similar to what teachers use in Tools of the Mind classrooms. I knew it was effective because my students' self-control skills improved exponentially after I implemented it. Students would repeatedly tell me how they "stopped to think about their actions" and how proud they felt to stick to a task even when they wanted to quit. With this kind of evidence, I wondered, could I use this template at home? I knew that around peers and teachers, most children work hard to control themselves and to act according to social norms. Home is different. It's a place for children to test boundaries and limits with family members. Taking this into account, I found alternative strategies that worked at home.

Introducing planning to Jacob (who was 4½ at the time) would certainly be different from how I did it in class. I was curious as to how he would respond to talking about his plan and how this might affect his actions and feelings. I realized that I rarely talked with him about what he planned to do. Often, he initiated his play, and when things did not go according to his idea, he would act out. At first, I tried to stop the outbursts by offering all sorts of incentives, but this was like putting a lid on boiling water. Eventually, the lid blew off. During his outbursts, I gave Jacob clear boundaries on where he could have a tantrum, told him he was not to break things, and then let him be. I gave him the chance to feel his anger and act on it, but I did not reflect on the incident with him.

# PLANNING TEMPLATE

## HOW TO PLAN WITH YOUR CHILD

Your template can be simple and feel fun. Think about using bold letters, playful frames, simple drawings, colorful paper, or fun stickers to help engage your child.

Invite your child to write or draw their idea

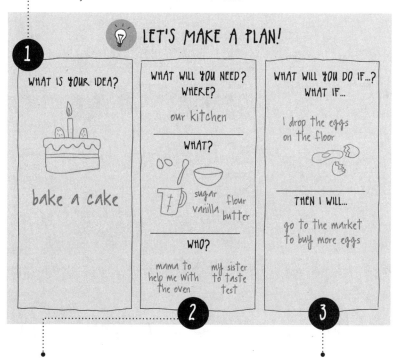

**LET'S MAKE A PLAN!**

**1**

WHAT IS YOUR IDEA?

bake a cake

WHAT WILL YOU NEED? WHERE?

our kitchen

WHAT?

sugar
vanilla flour
butter

WHO?

mama to help me with the oven

my sister to taste test

WHAT WILL YOU DO IF...? WHAT IF...

I drop the eggs on the floor

THEN I WILL...

go to the market to buy more eggs

**2**

**3**

**Where:** what part of the home will your child use? Where will your child play?

**What:** what materials do you need to make your child's idea happen?

**Who:** Does your child's idea need someone else to help? Ask *whether* and *how* they want to join in.

Most things don't go according to plan so anticipate/plan for change.

 Make your own template

Figure 4

# REFLECTION TEMPLATE

## HOW TO REFLECT WITH YOUR CHILD

- Listen to your child and help record their thoughts with simple drawings to illustrate their thinking.
- Invite your child to draw or write, you can scribe if needed.
- Avoid judgement.

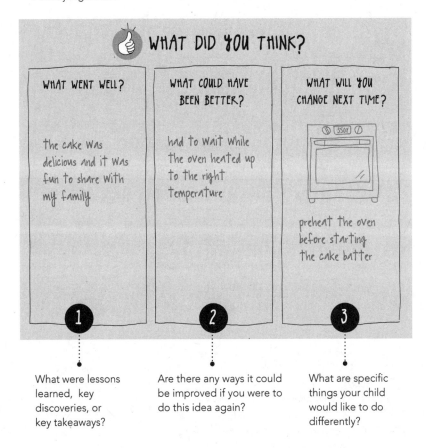

**WHAT DID YOU THINK?**

**WHAT WENT WELL?**

the cake was delicious and it was fun to share with my family

**WHAT COULD HAVE BEEN BETTER?**

had to wait while the oven heated up to the right temperature

**WHAT WILL YOU CHANGE NEXT TIME?**

preheat the oven before starting the cake batter

**1**

What were lessons learned, key discoveries, or key takeaways?

**2**

Are there any ways it could be improved if you were to do this idea again?

**3**

What are specific things your child would like to do differently?

 Make your own template

Figure 5

I chose to talk with Jacob about planning after dinner. We discussed, in detail, what he was going to do before bath time. Normally, I used that time to clean up and sort out the kitchen. To be honest, I felt some frustration that I was going to lose some of my cleanup time to talking with him and questioned whether I was wasting my time. Would this avoid the evening meltdown? Entering this conversation with doubt was probably going to sabotage my plan. I breathed into my doubt and waited until I felt more optimistic, then asked, "So, what are you going to do before it's time to brush your teeth? What's your play plan?"

He stopped, looked at me, and then answered, "I'm going to play with my LEGOs."

I asked, "Oh, do you have any ideas about what you'll build?"

He paused again. "I want to build a garage for my race cars."

I responded, "Oh, a garage. How many race cars can fit in the garage?"

I could see Jacob thinking. The seed had been planted about the size—I wanted him to visualize the dimensions. "So, what if the garage doesn't turn out as you plan? Imagine, for example, that all of your cars don't fit in the garage. What will you do?" I wondered if he could tell I was asking about how he would handle his frustration.

"I'll make a smaller garage for the other cars."

I decided to be very explicit. "If it still doesn't work, will you slam the garage on the ground? Or will you try to pause and take a breath, or even walk away and ask for help if you need it?"

I offered him some ideas on how he might manage his anger, and to my surprise, he listened. Then I said, "Sounds like a great plan. Have fun! Oh, and if you become frustrated, I'll come to see you once you've quieted down. I become angry when I see you frustrated. I don't want to put my anger on you." I'd specified the boundaries and also shared my feelings with him. Then I looked at the clock and said he had about an hour to play before it was time to brush his teeth. Telling him the time let him know there was a time limit for his play. Often, children do not want to stop playing when they are asked, so telling them there is a time limit helps; even if they can't yet tell time, they understand that there is a limit to their playtime.

After all that talk, there was still an outburst. I heard a holler and then a loud crash. This time, however, Jacob calmed himself faster. When I peeked into the room to see if he was okay, he looked sad and said, "The garage was bad." I responded, "Oh." I did not shame him for not controlling his actions. It was too soon to talk with him about what had happened. We would reflect later that night.

After tucking Jacob into bed, I asked if I could tell the story about his plan. I drew out the incident on a piece of paper with stick figures and crude shapes. It showed us talking and him building in his room. Then I paused. I asked him to tell the part of the story when he threw the LEGO bricks. I drew as he spoke, and he watched me. We talked about the moment that he threw his LEGO bricks, his frustration, and that he took a breath to calm himself. We talked more about his anger. I could sense he was gaining some awareness of how to pause before reacting.

This personal incident illustrates the value of taking the time to talk with your child about their plans, ideas, and intentions. To regularly implement this, work the following steps into your activities as you go about your day.

**Check in with your child in between routines.** There will be natural transitions during the day. They usually occur around routines, such as morning, meals, and bedtime. Let your child know ahead of time that a transition will be coming. Before and after these predictable times afford chances to talk with your child about their intentions, plans, outcomes, and reflections.

**Ask your child what they will do next and the anticipated outcome.** Talk with your child about their intentions. Help them identify the materials they might need (if any) to complete their task. Consider the level of skill needed to achieve their goal and compare it to their current level of skill.

**Troubleshoot together before initiating the plan and clearly define boundaries.** The aim is to elicit unexpected outcomes so they can mentally prepare for them. Discuss boundaries together in advance, making clear what is and is not acceptable.

**Reflect together.** After completion, talk about how things went. Discuss what worked well and determine changes for the future. Consider reflecting together through drawing. This can help your child see their plan, the cause and effect of their actions, and their thoughts. On a piece of paper, use simple stick-figure drawings to highlight their thinking, which helps children "see" what they are thinking.

To reflect on their actions, your child needs to remember the experience. This highlights an important distinction related to memory development: the difference between *semantic* and *episodic* memory. Semantic memory allows us to remember facts about the world (for example, Disneyland is in California), whereas episodic memory relates to remembering personal experiences, including sometimes "traveling back in time" to reexperience those events (like meeting Mickey Mouse in Disneyland). Children start talking about past events around 2 years of age,[48] but many researchers argue that episodic memory is not fully developed until at least 4 years of age.[49,50]

One way that researchers have examined young children's understanding of the past and their ability to reexperience it is with a fun, simple game.[51] In this "sticker game," 2-, 3-, and 4-year-olds are videotaped as they play with an adult experimenter. During the activity, the adult covertly places a small sticker on the child's forehead. A few minutes later, the child watches the video (while the sticker is still on their head), including the key segment when the sticker is placed on their head. The researchers found that (while the sticker is still on their head) most of the 2- and 3-year-olds did not reach up and remove the sticker from their head, but the majority of the 4-year-olds did. These findings suggest that children younger than 4 years of age often struggle to understand their role in past events (like recognizing themselves in a video) and how that relates to current experiences.

The next time you ask your child to think about their behavior, be easy on them. It could be that, developmentally, they are unable to recall the incident the way you think they should. If they happen to reflect on the experience, don't be surprised if a few days later they can't remember what they said. As you think about ways to support your child's memory development, consider these reflection questions:

- How have you heard your child talk about a past event? Have they developed episodic memory?

- Ask your child to tell you a story about a positive memory that you shared. Then share your own memory of that time. How are the memories the same? How are they different?

## Building EF at Different Ages

For children under 4 years old, it helps to model for them how to plan and reflect. As mentioned above, they might not be developmentally ready to do this on their own, but it's never too early to model important skills. As you have learned from the previous chapters, one of the ways children learn is by watching, listening to, and imitating what they see. Here are some key concepts to focus on when building your child's EF muscles, accompanied by age-appropriate recommendations based on developmental stage.

**Provide choice and give children agency when possible.**

- *Infants:* Hold up two foods or toys and let them choose by pointing or reaching toward their preference.

- *Toddlers:* Let them take part in family decisions; if you're taking an outing to the zoo, for example, let them decide which animals to see and in what order.

- *Preschoolers:* Give children access to craft materials or building blocks, then let them decide what to create and how to make it.

- *School-age children:* Capitalize on a child's interests by watching related videos, reading books, making creations, and engaging in play around those interests.

**Encourage free play, especially pretend play.**

- *Infants:* Notice how your child can lead, even as a baby (for example, notice which toy your infant reaches for), and support their investigations when they need assistance.

- *Toddlers:* Provide props to support pretend play (dolls, blankets, cars) and narrate what is happening as your child plays.

- *Preschoolers:* Avoid overscheduling structured activities (music lessons, organized sports) and instead value the times when your child uses their imagination to transform themselves and their environment.

- *School-age children:* Continue to allow and encourage pretend play and child-directed play into the elementary years.

**Give children opportunities and support to plan and reflect.**

- *Infants:* Notice and narrate when they achieve their intended goal, like crawling across the room to retrieve a toy.

- *Toddlers:* Offer the opportunity to make a simple plan, such as deciding on the last thing they want to do before leaving the playground.

- *Preschoolers:* After stating their goal, such as making a cat with craft materials, help them think through the details of their plan, such as the body parts of a cat and which materials they will need to make each part.

- *School-age children:* After finishing a project, have a conversation about what went well and what they could do even better.

## Strengthen Your EF Muscles Too

Too often, we parents feel frustrated by our children's developing EF skills, but we forget that they are watching our actions and listening to what we say to learn how to respond to the world around them. My son, Jacob, the one with the fiery temper and lack of patience, was learning about inhibition, self-control, and cognitive flexibility from me. It's hard to admit this, but it's true. At first, I sat around blaming others for his behavior, thinking, *Ugh, he's just like my mom!* or *I have to change preschools—he learns the worst things there!* Then one day I heard him talking to his trains. "What is wrong with you?" he asked the caboose. It was the same question I'd asked my husband the night before when I yelled at him, in front of our children, for putting his wet umbrella on the dining room table.

My EF muscles, particularly my self-control, needed strengthening! I was moving a hundred miles an hour, reacting to everything that came my way, without pausing to think about what I was saying and who else was listening.

When I heard my son parroting my words, I realized (much to my horror) that he wasn't behaving like my mother or a child from his preschool; he was copying me. In child development, we often refer to this process as *co-regulating*. Co-regulating involves paying close attention to how children are understanding and expressing their thoughts and feelings, responding consistently and sensitively with the right level of support, and modeling how to regulate behavior.[52]

I was careful to co-regulate with my students, but not as careful at home. In the classroom, I was constantly evaluating my behavior, making sure that what I modeled reflected the actions I wanted to see from my students. I spent time watching their cues so that I would respond to their needs in a manner that suited their individual temperaments. For example, 3-year-old Josie was quite shy, so when I approached her hiding in the library corner of the classroom, I made sure that my actions were slow and that my tone of voice was softer than usual. At home, I wasn't doing any of this. Around my family, I was distracted and reactive. I forgot to pay attention to my children's cues, especially Jacob's. I knew he had a fiery temperament, and when he lost control, my fiery temper met his. You, too, might notice that when you are with your colleagues, and even strangers, your interactions are more intentional, warm, and responsive than they are with your family.

To strengthen your own EF muscles at home, think about the concept of co-regulating. Ask yourself: *What behavior do I want to make regular in the household?* Take a moment to sit quietly and recall a recent interaction with your child that you regret. If you journal, write out the story line of the incident and the thoughts that accompany it. First, notice the subtle physical sensations that you feel in your body when you recall the interaction. If there's judgment or shame, put it aside for a moment. The process of reflecting objectively, noting the past, and asking how you can grow breeds wisdom and change.

So build your EF skills by replaying the incident as objectively as you can, pondering the following questions.

*About your child's actions:*

- What messages were your child's body language and tone of voice sending? Were they the same or different from what was being said?

- What were they communicating? How were they expressing their needs?

- When do you usually see this type of behavior? Is there a specific time of day or stimulus that often precedes breakdowns (like school pickup, after screen time, in between meals)? What patterns do you notice from the behavior?

- Do you see yourself in your child's actions? Are your temperaments similar?

*About your actions:*

- How can you use this opportunity to co-regulate?

- In addition to what you were saying, what messages were you sending your child (through body language, tone of voice, and actions)? When did you feel you'd reached your limit and why?

- What can you do differently in the future to respond more sensitively and consistently? Replay the incident again, this time seeing yourself co-regulating in a new way. How does it feel to try a different approach?

Be patient. There will be days when you'll forget to read your child's cues. This is normal; try to avoid self-judgment. Observing, reflecting, planning, and making incremental changes to your behavior are the best ways to strengthen your EF muscles. In part two of the book, you'll learn how to inquire about your child's actions, listen to their responses with respect, and be aware of your assumptions about why they do what

The Emotionally Intelligent Child

they do—a practice that strengthens your ability to successfully observe, reflect, and change. When you combine this practice with your knowledge of EF skills, your family will co-regulate, grow, and thrive together.

As you've learned in this chapter, building your child's EF skills provides a strong foundation for their emotional intelligence, allowing them to pause, focus their attention, plan, and remember their intentions. In other words, EF provides a structure to your child's thinking that allows them to positively engage with others. Your child's EF skills develop with your support and encouragement through conversations, play, everyday routines, and how you structure your child's time.

So far in the book, as we've highlighted your child's social-emotional development, a question may have crossed your mind: How does social-emotional development differ among families with parents who have different values and parenting styles? In the next chapter, we explore how your family culture and compassionate relationships support and shape your child's social-emotional learning.

# CHAPTER 4

# Develop Compassion Within Your Family Culture

At the start of the school year, Terrance (3½ years) sobbed every day at snack time and refused to eat the cold apple slices that the school provided. Nadia (4 years) hid in the bathroom with the fire hat from the dress-up box. I did not know the children well enough yet to understand their behavior, but I figured there had to be something more to what I was seeing because it happened daily. Based on my experience teaching children from many different cultures at international schools in both China and the US, I started to wonder whether Terrance's and Nadia's behaviors were shaped by cultural traditions from home. This was a challenging conversation to have with preschoolers, so I made a conscious effort to get to know their families better. When I asked their families, Terrance's mom shared that she was taught by her Chinese family that cold food was hard for the body to digest and might make you sick. That helped to explain why Terrance cried when he was told to eat his snack—he believed the cold apples would make him sick. After talking with Nadia's grandmother, her behavior made more sense too. Grandma told me, "Don't let Nadia dress up like a fireman at school. That's not a girl's job." Grandma was an elderly woman from eastern Europe with her own cultural views on gender roles and jobs. Nadia wanted to dress in all the costumes, like the rest of the children, so she hid in the bathroom to play dress-up.

In this chapter, you will see how family culture and compassionate relationships support and shape children's social and emotional learning. It is important to clarify what we mean by the term "family culture" because culture has many accepted uses and meanings. Cross-cultural psychology, for example, refers to how cultural factors influence behavior, often comparing European and North American cultures to those of other parts of the world. In this book, we use culture in the context of family to refer to the specific values, traditions, and norms that encompass your family's way of thinking, feeling, judging, and acting. We are all shaped by the family culture into which we are born or raised. For example, if you come from a family that makes a big deal of birthdays, then you might be disappointed when your friend or partner doesn't get you a birthday gift.

Like the developing child, family culture is always growing and transitioning. Each member of the family perceives the world in their own way, through their cycles of development. And the family as a whole develops collectively. Situations within families change, such as birth, death, and illness; and larger external forces, like society, politics, economics, and technology, further influence family culture, requiring the family to adapt. It is inevitable that events and circumstances will challenge your family norms, which is why compassion is needed to keep your family culture thriving.

Consider what you have learned so far about your child's developmental progressions of theory of mind, language and communication, and executive function, noting that these continuums are, in part, affected by your family culture and the compassionate nature of your relationships.

Nadia's and Terrance's beliefs and behaviors, like those of most children, have been largely molded by their family culture. This is not a new idea. In the 1920s, psychologist Lev Vygotsky argued that children's understanding of the world is shaped through social interactions with adults and other children.[53,54] In other words, children do not develop in an isolated vacuum; they are part of a multifaceted and ever-evolving world. Vygotsky's sociocultural theory of development emphasizes that as children play and cooperate with others, they learn what is important to members of their culture and society. Your child thinks and behaves based on what they are taught, and oftentimes, these lessons are passed on through your family's words and actions. If your child is raised with extended family nearby, for instance, they may have a different concept of "family" (grandparents who are part of birthday and holiday celebrations) than a child whose relatives live far away. Family culture helps lay the foundation for how and what your child learns.

## Mapping the Influencers Beyond Your Family Culture

"Influencers" is a term we often hear in social media, but we're going to use it to talk about child development. In this case, influencers are the people your child looks to for guidance, growth, and safety. In addition to family members, there are always other people who influence your child. You cannot control these influencers, but you can prepare for the ways in which you will react to how they're influencing your child. There will always be a multitude of influencers in your child's life—for example, people living in your home, extended family, friends, teachers, coaches, and sitters. In addition, your child will be influenced by social media posters as they grow older. These influencers each have their own past experiences and cultural traditions that shaped their beliefs and actions, which in turn shape your child's.

Consider the story of 4-year-old Robert. He returned from his play-date with Jonah upset and confused. "I'm never going to eat lunch at Jonah's house again because he won't let me drink milk. He said we aren't allowed to drink milk with our food. I drink milk every day with my lunch. Why did Jonah say it's bad to drink milk with my turkey sandwich? Isn't drinking milk good for you?" Robert was angry. At that moment, Robert's mom, Karen, realized Jonah's family kept kosher, but she didn't think to mention this possibility to Robert before the play-date. Now she needed to comfort Robert and explain that Jonah was not trying to be mean but was following his family's religious traditions for eating meals. More importantly, she wanted to make sure that Robert would grow up to accept people's differences. Robert needed to know that families are unique and that they follow norms, beliefs, and values that reflect their family culture.

The concept of influencers is captured in Urie Bronfenbrenner's bioecological approach to development, which considers a child's environments as multiple aspects or systems—from immediate contexts like the home and school to broad cultural customs and laws—that interact in complex ways to shape children's development.[55] More specifically, a child's "microsystem" includes the roles and relationships that directly impact the child in their daily lives and may include parents and siblings, peers, teachers, and neighbors. Importantly, Bronfenbrenner stresses the bidirectional nature of those relationships. For instance, a child's behavior can have an impact on their parents' relationship, and the parents' relationship, in turn, can affect how they interact with their child. Another "layer" of influence is the "macrosystem," which represents broad cultural influences (governments, religion, political values). For example, many cultures value education, which impacts the views and practices of people living in that society.

To think systematically about your child's influencers, it helps to map them. The following exercise is influenced by Bronfenbrenner's work to help you think about the different layers and systems of influencers in your child's life.

1.  Draw a circle in the center of a piece of paper with lines coming out like a sun with rays.

2.  In the center of the circle, write your child's name. Then, at the end of each ray, write the name of an influencer (Grandma Rose, Mr. Huffman [teacher]).

3.  Circle the names at the end of the rays and then draw rays extending out from these circles. At the end of these rays, write their influencers. (It will look something like figure 6.)

# INFLUENCER MAP

## WHO INFLUENCES, AFFECTS, AND SUPPORTS YOUR CHILD?

CULTURE    VALUES    CUSTOMS & BELIEFS    LAWS & RULES    RESOURCES    ENVIRONMENT

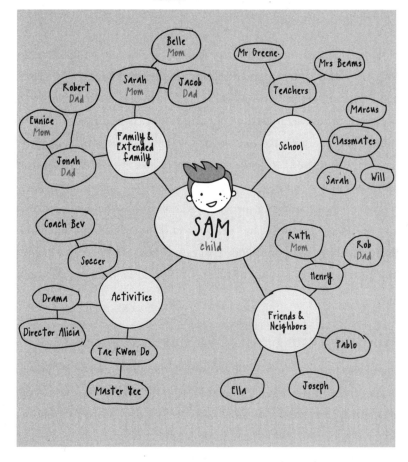

 Make your own map

Figure 6

4. Consider the systems that shape the influencers' thinking, such as their culture, values, customs and beliefs, laws and rules, resources, and environment in order to reflect on how these structures influence behavior.

5. Use the habits of a systems thinker to understand how your child is developing and being influenced. Systems thinkers consider the big picture of what could be influencing something or someone and the cause and effect of those relationships.[56]

When you look at your influencer map, you may be surprised to see how many circles and rays you drew. Identifying influencers and reflecting on their different cultures, values, and the bidirectional nature of their relationships helps clarify your child's understanding of the world around them and prepares you for the conversations you will have with your child when they ask about the practices and views that differ from your own family culture.

There will always be influencers and conditions that will challenge your parenting intentions and get your child questioning their family culture. Keeping these influencers in mind, take the time to explicitly think about your family values and how you will teach and model them.

## Building Your Family Values Inventory

When I was teaching preschool, during the parents' meeting at the start of each school year, I asked each parent to rank a list of character traits they valued. Our classroom was like a family with core values, and we worked as a team to build them, being careful of how we influenced one another. Importantly, I wanted to be sure to include the core values of each student's family into the classroom, even if they differed.

I asked parents to select five character traits that were important to them and rank them in order, with number one being the most important. The goal was for everyone to do an internal audit of their values.

I suggest you take the time to do this too. Here's the list of character traits the parents in my class used to make their choices. What are your top five?

- *Acceptance:* having an open mind toward others' ideas and practices, even if they differ from yours

- *Compassion:* understanding that you and/or others will suffer and wanting to do something to help

- *Courage:* willingness to try difficult things

- *Equality:* believing that everyone deserves the same respect and rights

- *Adaptability:* being flexible, able to change plans and ideas when needed

- *Fairness:* acting in a just way and sharing or behaving accordingly

- *Generosity:* willingness to share and give resources to help others

- *Honesty:* being truthful and sincere

- *Integrity:* acting according to your moral and ethical principles

- *Kindness:* being considerate and treating others well

- *Respect:* considering the worth of something or someone and treating it or them with the value in mind

- *Open-mindedness:* listening to other people and respecting their ideas

- *Perseverance:* persisting through challenge

- *Politeness:* behaving according to social norms; using good manners

- *Responsibility:* being reliable

- *Self-control:* staying calm and managing your actions and words

- *Other:* identify and explain

If you do this exercise with your parenting partner, keep in mind it is normal to have some values that differ. After all, you had different influencers. The goal of this exercise is to carefully consider how you would like to influence your child, being mindful of your social interactions. Naming your values and talking about them with your co-parent helps align your intentions and provides a North Star for how you will influence your child.

## Family Culture Shapes Compassion

One of the main reasons we think about influencers and take time to identify and model our values for children is because we want to teach them how to be *compassionate*, or how to care for others. Karen Armstrong, a thought leader on compassion, says that to make compassion actionable, we can think of it like the Golden Rule—we should treat others as we wish to be treated ourselves.[57] According to Armstrong in her TED Talk titled "Let's Revive the Golden Rule," when we interact with others, we have to look into our hearts to see what gives us pain and then refuse to inflict that pain on others. Already, you have shown your compassion by reading this book and by taking the time to reflect on your parenting style. There is no doubt that you want to raise a kind and compassionate child.

Compassion takes time for your child to develop, and your family culture shapes your child's view of it. For example, when showing acts of compassion, maybe your family culture prompts you to get physically close to others when you see them in distress. One day you and your child witness an elderly individual fall in a parking lot. To offer help to this person, you bend down and reach out your hand to help them up. The fallen individual, however, snaps, "Don't get too close to me," and your child looks at you confused. Let your child know that compassionate actions differ depending on family culture. In chapter 1 on ToM, we talked about how your child builds their social understanding in part from the emotional expressions and responses of their family and other influencers. Compassionate actions differ, but the end goal is the same: to not inflict pain or hurt on others. Most family cultures value kindness and compassion, and there are ways to explicitly foster your child's compassion and ways you can model it.

Compassion is crucial to emotional intelligence. It breeds kindness, forgiveness, and acceptance; however, we can't talk about compassion without talking about *empathy*. Empathy and compassion are closely related concepts—empathy is the ability to sense or imagine what someone else is thinking or feeling, whereas compassion includes the desire to help.[58] Children need to build both. Interestingly, research finds that the two concepts are represented in different areas of the brain; empathy activates parts of the brain linked to self-awareness and emotion, and compassion stimulates activity in areas connected to learning and decision making.[59] Chapter 3 addressed how to build the muscles of executive function—the same can be done with empathy and compassion. Research by neuroscientists has shown that empathy and compassion are skills that can be taught and nurtured, and training programs have demonstrated increases in prosocial behavior.[60,61]

Maddie, a preschooler in my classroom, and her family introduced me to a game they played to nurture empathy and compassion. Maddie had a deep social intuition and a remarkable skill to notice the energy and emotions of other children. She could enter the pretend world of her peers without ruffling feathers by watching them play make-believe games and offering to take on a role they picked for her. Children wanted to play with Maddie because she was responsive to their needs and moods. When I mentioned this to her parents, they looked at each other with a smile and said it must be from the game they play before bed.

"A game?" I asked. "Tell me more." Maddie's parents wanted their children to think about and care for the family, as well as for others outside of their home, so they made up a game using photos of family, friends, and strangers. In the game, they took turns imagining they were each person in the picture to help their kids think about others with empathy. If the photos showed someone needing help, Maddie's parents asked her to think about what she might do to show compassion. At 5 years old, Maddie was the perfect age to play this game because she had a basic understanding of ToM and the perspective-taking skills that are critical components of empathy and compassion. This game is appropriate for children who are just starting to talk and older.

Here's how you can play this picture game at home to build your own child's empathy and compassion skills:

1. *Before* you play, set boundaries for the game (and follow through with them), such as, "We'll look at a picture before tonight's bedtime story." This can help avoid common bedtime conflicts when it is getting late but your child wants to continue playing.

2. Choose a group picture of the family (a printed photo or one on your phone). For example, the photo may show your child being pushed on the swings by her father while her grandmother sits nearby with the family dog. The goal of the conversation is to build compassion, so a photo showing various facial expressions or actions would be ideal.

3. Begin promoting empathy by asking your child to take the perspective of the people in the photo by thinking about their thoughts, feelings, and actions without judgment. Wonder out loud about the people in the photo. Take time

to talk about what you see in the picture, including context, to remind your child that people act in certain ways depending on factors like location and time.

4.  Next, pretend to be someone in the photo and communicate what you are thinking and feeling as that person. If someone in the photo looks unhappy or uneasy, ask your child what could be done to help them.

A sample dialogue in this exercise might go like this:

*Parent:*  Before your bedtime story tonight, let's play a game. I'll find a photo, and we'll pretend to be everyone in the photo. I'll pretend to be Daddy. Hmm, what is he thinking and feeling here? Maybe he's thinking, "I like being at the park with *(name of your child)*. Oh, this swing goes high. My legs are getting tired from standing and pushing the swing. *(Make Dad's tummy grumble.)* I feel a little hungry. I wonder if Sampson *(point to the dog)* is hungry too? I'll give him a little extra food when we get home."

*Child:*  *(Laughing)* It's my turn.

*Parent:*  Okay, who are you going to be? *(Your child might choose themselves or copy what you said, and that's fine—it helps them build a sense of self. After they talk about themselves, ask if they would like another turn to imagine being someone else. Your child might need a few prompts to get started, such as, "Would you like to pretend to be Grandma now?" Once you have helped, your job is to listen and let your child do the talking.)*

*Child:*  I'll be Grandma. She's thinking, "I like coming to the park because I like to watch the birds. I am sitting on the bench with Sampson. I have to hold Sampson so he doesn't chase the birds."

*Parent:*    What if Sampson runs to chase a bird? What would she say to Sampson when he chases the birds? What if Sampson pulls Grandma off when he chases the bird? How would you help her?

At the end of the game, explain to your child that you really can't know what another person is thinking or feeling unless you ask them, but it's good to practice imagining how someone thinks and feels because it shows you care about them.

## Modeling Compassion in Ways That Suit Your Style

In addition to playing games with your child to build empathy and compassion, you need to model it. You may have discovered that modeling compassion takes effort. Clayton was reminded of this most mornings. He looked at his watch, breathed a sigh of relief, and thought that this might be a morning without a meltdown. No sooner had he finished his thought than the crying began. Aria (3½ years old) sat in the hall, screaming and pounding her fists on the floor. "No, no, Daddy, no!" she wailed. "I can't wear these socks. They're not green. I want the green ones." She was inconsolable. The cat fled the room. Clayton wished he could follow the cat, but he had to get Aria to school. He glanced at the clock; he couldn't be late for work.

Clayton had five minutes to resolve the sock situation. His chest tightened while the anger rose. He paused. He wasn't going to respond the way he did yesterday, raising his voice and demanding that Aria stop crying. Clayton shook his hands, wiggled his fingers, and opened and closed his palms. This helped—it cooled him down and created some space for the anger. He knew that Aria needed compassion, but he wasn't ready to deal with her yet. His parenting style was more demanding and less tolerant, especially when he needed to get to work. Over time, Clayton realized that even though he didn't always understand Aria's outbursts, when he responded to her with patience and compassion, she calmed down fast.

Most children calm down when they feel safe, accepted, validated, and cared for. In essence, they need to feel your compassion. It's natural for your child to sometimes cry and behave irrationally, like Aria wanting her green socks. It's also natural for you to occasionally feel frustrated and confused by your child's behavior. Clayton told himself to think of Aria's tears as a cry for compassion. What Aria was really saying was, *Every morning I'm a little scared to leave you, Dad. I panic when it's time for school and worry about being without you. Let me know that you care, Dad, and that you will always be here to help.*

To parent with compassion, it helps to know your parenting style. Keep two things in mind:

1. Parenting styles are determined by a balance of responsiveness and demandingness. Responsiveness is shown by being warm, attuned, and supportive, while demandingness shows your response to behavior, the consequences for unacceptable actions, and your follow-through.

2. Parenting styles are deeply influenced by your family culture. Family culture helps us decide which behavior is acceptable, the limits of acceptance, and how to control unacceptable behavior.

Keep compassion at the core of your family culture and determine how your parenting style will balance responsiveness and demandingness.

In the 1960s, Diana Baumrind, a developmental psychologist at the University of California at Berkeley, theorized that there is a close connection between parenting styles and children's behavior, and her work is still being referenced today.[62] One key question for developmental researchers is how differences in parenting styles influence the well-being and development of children. Baumrind classified parenting into three types, and a fourth was later added to her framework. Based on her research, the style parents should aim for is finding the right balance between responsiveness and demandingness. When the scale tips too much toward one side or the other, you should pause and readjust your balance. You may see a little bit of yourself in each of the parenting styles Baumrind identified, which might worry you at first. In part two, you'll learn some techniques to help you remain balanced. For now, let's take a look at these styles, and as you read about them, think about past experiences when you have leaned heavily toward each. What was the circumstance? What steps did you take to return to balance?

**Authoritative parenting.** This parenting style tends to be warm and responsive, with clear rules and boundaries. Although parents value independence, they also have high expectations for behavior and follow through with consequences. These parents often reason with their children and are successful communicators. This can be seen, for example, when a parent and a child negotiate an acceptable bedtime and why. This style weighs responsiveness and demandingness equally on the balance scale. Imagine yourself parenting in this style. How do you think your child will respond? Will they feel your compassion?

**Authoritarian parenting.** This parenting style can be viewed as strict and unforgiving. Parents have high expectations for appropriate behavior and prefer their children to be more obedient than independent. Being warm and responsive is not their immediate reaction. Instead, they favor a less responsive, more demanding style, with an "I told you so" tone of voice. An example of this would be a parent responding with "Because I say so" when their child asks why they are being punished. This style tips the balance scale toward demandingness. When you are overly demanding, how does your child respond? How do you feel afterward?

**Permissive parenting.** Permissive parents are warm and responsive to their children, but they tend to be lenient with their rules and more indulgent. For example, a permissive parent may not ask their child where they are going or when they will be back as their child runs out the door to play with neighborhood friends. The scale here is tipped toward responsiveness. How does your child respond when you don't make any demands of them? When you need to make a demand, how do they react?

**Uninvolved parenting.** This parenting style did not originate from Baumrind's research, but was added later by psychologists Eleanor Maccoby and John Martin.[63] This style is both the least responsive and the least demanding. These parents tend to be indifferent to their child's behavior and may have little knowledge of what their children are doing. It is difficult to find balance in this style because, in essence, there is no scale. How do you think your child will learn your family values if you parent this way?

As we saw with Clayton, Aria, and the green socks, Clayton initially leaned toward an authoritarian style, but then noticed he needed to adjust his response and demands to help his daughter calm down. Clayton found success when he was responsive to her needs, showing patience and curiosity but still demanding that she put her socks on.

To keep your parenting style balanced between responding with warmth and care while still demanding that your child follow your family values, here are some points to remember:

- Tune in to how you respond to your child and what you demand from them. Regulating your own behavior is as important as teaching your child to regulate their behavior. In chapter 5 on mindfulness, you will learn techniques to do this.

- Warm and supportive responses to your child's actions can foster a sense of safety and closeness. Supportive responses summarize how a child feels, such as, "It looks like you're feeling angry that you can't find the puzzle piece," in contrast to, "If you kept the pieces in the box, one wouldn't be missing now." The latter comment shames the child, and who wants to be shamed? We'll talk more about shame and judgment in chapter 7.

- Make sure you can follow through with the consequences you set. If you say, "If you don't finish your dinner, you'll never get dessert," ask yourself whether you are ready to *never* give dessert to your child again.

- Be sensitive to context. Some days your child might need you to be more responsive and less demanding. Modify your style to meet your child's needs in the moment. The follow-through on consequences can happen later. For instance, be warm and supportive at the time of a sensitive incident, then later that day, when your child is more centered, you can discuss the consequences of their actions. We'll present examples of how to do this in chapter 8.

## A Child's View of Family

As you clarify your family culture, consider how your child might perceive it. Children are perceptive and sense their family values by watching their family and other influencers, often imitating what they see. I once overheard children in the after-school gardening club (for 4- to 7-year-olds) talking. Felix and Yuan Xin had decided that they were the parents to the cucumber plants. They gleefully declared, "We are the cucumber family!" The other children in the club thought this was a good idea, and in no time, additional families were formed. Adaku and William were the parents to the tomatoes (with twenty-one tomato children and counting!); Ayden and Mira raised eight butternut squash; and so on. The children would care for the garden, making sure the basic needs of their "plant children" were met. Did the plants have enough water? How many hours of sunlight were they getting? Did the "plant parents" need to add more plant food to the soil? Lastly, were there any pests or "bullies" (as the children called them) that were harming the plants' growth? The children talked with one another to find out how their plant families were doing, sharing tips the same way their own parents shared parenting advice. At times, they would tell a friend that their vegetable children were naughty: "I need to remind them to be polite. They are hogging all the sun!" Through their play and conversations, children share their family values with one another. Your child is an influencer too!

As your child develops, they are eager to share with other children what they learn from you and the other influencers in their life. In an effort to make friends, children tend to watch what another child is doing before approaching them. If they perceive that the other child is doing something interesting (which might not match what you find interesting), that it seems fun and safe to play with, they then try to connect. During her toddler years, my daughter, Nina, stood at the end of the playground slide and clapped for select kids as they came down. She would not clap for the kid who cut in line or the kid who shoved his brother out of the way so he could go first. In no time, she toddled over to one of the kids she'd clapped for and joined their play. How does your child choose playmates? What actions or qualities does your child find appealing? Taking the time to notice this will help you understand what your child is looking for in a friend or what they want to learn in that moment.

Young children begin looking to connect with others during the first few months of life. Research has shown that even infants can distinguish between positive and negative actions toward others. In one study, 5- and 9-month-old infants were introduced to several puppets— some that were helpful and others that were not.[64] The infants watched as one of the puppets reached out to help another that was struggling to open a box with an attractive toy inside (the "opener") while a second puppet jumped on the lid of the box, slamming it shut (the "closer"). After the show, the infants were offered the chance to reach for and look to both the opener and closer puppets. The infants overwhelmingly preferred the puppet that behaved prosocially (the opener) and avoided the antisocial one (the closer).

These findings suggest that well before their first birthday, infants pay attention to and prefer those who may help. One way to distinguish those who may help from those who may harm is by observing how people treat others. For example, your child observes cooperative gestures, which encourages them to know how to connect with others. Knowing how to connect, your child is on their way to understanding cooperation—a fundamental skill of emotional intelligence.

## How Puppet Play Can Teach Family Values

Using puppets is a great tool for modeling your family values and is a fun and interactive way to build prosocial skills and practice identifying emotions. I discovered the power of puppets when I first began teaching 3- to 5-year-old preschoolers. One year, I had a class of children that fought with one another all the time. No matter how often I spoke with them about friendship, my words didn't sink in. That same year, a class parent donated a puppet theater to the class, which delighted the children to no end.

Watching the children play with the puppets, I wondered how they would respond if they saw their own behavior portrayed through the puppets, treating others in ways that were unfair or unkind. Would the children offer advice on how to change their own behavior when the puppets imitated them? Would seeing the puppets act out the children's behavior promote more prosocial behaviors among my students? I planned a puppet show for the children. The idea was to first use the puppets to show the children their social conflicts, then have the puppets interact with the kids and ask them questions. The results were miraculous. The children talked with the puppets about important topics, such as how to be a good friend, how to resolve conflicts, and the importance of kindness and honesty. The more time the children spent teaching the puppets, the more they demonstrated those positive behaviors in the classroom.

Within weeks, the children began listening to one another with more curiosity, patience, and kindness instead of quickly rejecting a peer's ideas. When I asked if they noticed a difference in their friendships, most of the children reported they felt happier. I took the idea home and used puppets with my own children (3 and 5 years old at the time). The puppets acted out scenes that mirrored my children's struggles, such as sharing their toys when a friend came to play. Interestingly, the results were the same: my children took the lessons they taught the puppets and applied them to their own behavior.

Puppet play provides an opportunity to safely show your child how one's actions can influence others. When you're the puppeteer, you want your child, when they are young, to learn to recognize your family values through the actions and emotions of the puppets. In addition, your child can identify and label the puppets' actions and feelings and talk with the puppets about positive ways to interact with others.

Here are some tips to create your own puppet shows:

1. Find puppets with mouths that can open and close. If you don't have access to actual puppets, old socks with button eyes (or eyes drawn in) will do. Stuffed animals can also work, but puppets are preferred because moving the mouth in different ways can depict more emotions.

2. Gather props for the puppets to interact with, such as toys, household items (like a spoon), and other items that your child uses frequently. Props make the show fun!

3. If you are stuck on ideas for your puppet show, refer back to the list of character traits you identified in your family

values inventory to act out. Show the value in action, then act out what the opposite looks like. For example, a puppet show on responsibility could have one puppet that arrives on time and follows through with what they say, while another is late and says one thing but does another. Ask your child what they think about this and what they might say to the puppets.

4. You do not have to be a talented puppeteer. It's okay if your child sees your mouth moving or if you don't have an actual puppet theater to hide behind. Children are forgiving. If you are having fun, your child will have fun too!

5. Kids can get very excited around puppet shows, so before the show begins, explain to your child how you expect "the audience" to behave. If you value sitting quietly when watching a show, for instance, then let your child know what your expectations are before the show. This way, you have set up guidelines, and if your child gets overly excited, you can pause to remind them of how to be an attentive audience.

6. Puppet shows don't have to be long or complicated. They can easily take the place of a bedtime story or an after-dinner family activity. Puppet shows are interactive and incredibly fun. Your child will enjoy seeing shows that reenact personal experiences that are familiar to them.

The power of puppet shows lies in what you are depicting, whether it's a social conflict or the inability to control one's impulses, shown in an exaggerated scenario to boost the fun. Here are some suggestions for age-appropriate puppet shows based on experience with preschool and early elementary classrooms. You are the best judge for what will work for your child, so adjust your show according to your child's needs and reactions in the moment.

# PUPPET PLAY

## SHOWING A FAMILY VALUE

TALK ABOUT THE PUPPET PLAY WITH YOUR CHILD

Figure 7

**Puppet shows for infants.** For this age group, contrast kind, helpful actions with unkind ones. Interact with the puppets by responding positively to the kind puppet and offering ways to help the unkind puppet. For instance, show one puppet sharing something with you and the other puppet trying to take something of yours. Talk to the puppets about their actions. To the second puppet, you might say, "Excuse me, this is my orange, but I'd be happy to share it with you. When we want something, instead of grabbing it, we say, 'May I have some orange, please?'"

**Puppet shows for toddlers.** When your child starts talking and answering questions, ask them to respond to what you've acted out. Questions like "Which puppet would you like to play with? Why?" help children reflect on the qualities to look for in a friend. Don't ignore the antisocial puppet or label it as bad. Instead, explain the prosocial behaviors that the puppet can engage in to be helpful and kind. You can also ask your child to tell the puppet how to connect with others. If your child needs some prompts, offer an A or B choice, such as, "Our puppet friend is struggling to open her box. Should we (A) offer to help or (B) laugh that she is not strong enough?" Follow up with, "What else can we do to help?" or "How would you like someone to help you?"

**Puppet shows for preschoolers.** Taking puppet shows to the next level, ask your child to put on a show with you. Give your child a puppet and take another for yourself. If you want to focus on a conflict your child has had with a friend at school or sharing toys with a sibling, be intentional about the scenes you reenact and the problem-solving strategies you reinforce. For instance, have one puppet work very hard to cook a healthy dinner and a second puppet complain, scream, and cry that they hate the dinner and refuse to eat it. Ask your child for suggestions on how to solve the problem, act out their proposed solution, and then debrief together on how their idea worked. Then perform the same story over again using a different strategy and ask your child to compare and contrast how the two solutions worked out. "What would solve the problem at dinner for one night? What's a different idea that might help solve the problem if the puppet acted that way every night?"

**Puppet shows for school-age children.** Even older children enjoy puppets. They're able to make up the lines for the puppets and put on shows for their younger siblings. You can watch as they become family influencers on behalf of the values you have instilled.

In this chapter, we've discussed how social forces shape child development. Namely, we talked about how there are a multitude of different influencers who directly and indirectly affect your child. On a related note, we talked about how you, as a parent, are one of the most prominent influencers in your child's life and, for that reason, why it's beneficial to reflect on your own parenting style. We also covered some ways to encourage healthy social development in your child, especially when it comes to empathy and compassion.

Ultimately, it is important to remember that your child is growing up in a huge world filled with social beings, and just as your child affects the people around them, they are also affected by the people who are a part of their own life. Helping your child navigate the world of influencers requires a parenting style that has the right balance between responsiveness and demandingness. Be patient with yourself and your child—there will be moments when your balance scale will tip too far in one direction, but you can consciously work to regain equilibrium.

Now that you have a broadened understanding of how your child's mind is developing, we're going to put that knowledge into practice in part two of the book. The chapters that follow will introduce you to the MIND framework—a tool to help you reflect on the developmental progression of how your child thinks about their emotions and social interactions and how to support your child's emotional growth.

# The MIND Framework

After reading part one, you have a deeper understanding that your child's development is a continuum of overlapping milestones and that it is difficult to isolate a single aspect of development, such as social-emotional learning, without considering other areas of growth. The ability for your child to think and reflect about their mental states—thoughts, emotions, desires, and beliefs—as well as the mental states of others, or theory of mind, develops over time and with your guidance. At the same time, your child is developing language and communication skills to effectively interact with others, refining executive function skills that support self-awareness and self-control, and navigating the cultural and social norms expected of them.

With a greater understanding of how the human mind develops, you can pause, relax, and settle into the joys of parenting. We offer the MIND framework to help you respond to your child by shifting your perspective to think how they think, or as we like to say, to get into your child's mind. Our framework is presented in themed chapters that correspond to the acronym—where MIND stands for mindfulness, inquiry, nonjudgment, and decide—providing steps you can take to support your child's social-emotional development. As you read chapters 5 through 8, you'll learn about each component of the framework and how to combine them into a comprehensive strategy to boost your child's social awareness and emotional intelligence.

# MIND FRAMEWORK

## HOW TO ALIGN WITH YOUR CHILD'S THOUGHTS & ACTIONS

### MINDFULNESS

*Paying attention to the present moment without judgment*

Being mindful puts you in the present moment so that you can attend to your child with ease. Taking time to observe your thoughts and feelings without immediately reacting to them makes a big difference when you are parenting.

### INQUIRY

*Pausing to gather information about your child's reaction*

Viewing the world like your child requires asking about their actions, listening to their responses with respect, and putting your assumptions about why they do what they do to the side.

### NON-JUDGMENT

*Not defaulting to shame, blame, and criticism*

Avoiding judgment by observing your child with respect to their development, their approach to experiences, and their needs.

### DECIDE

*Thinking about your response and making it intentional*

Being intentional about how you respond to your child's actions and noting your reactions will help shape your child's thinking and beliefs.

Figure 8

The Emotionally Intelligent Child

# CHAPTER 5

# Mindfulness Helps You Be Present with Your Child

Jane peeked into the classroom and saw her 3½-year-old daughter, Charlotte, sitting still during the class's good-bye routine. Soon Charlotte would be dismissed and the chaos would start. Jane felt the tension in her body and thought to herself, *This is crazy. It's like I'm afraid of my child.*

Ms. Fieldstone called out the names of the students one by one. Charlotte, eager to please her teacher, sat patiently until her name was called. When it was her turn, she calmly gathered her things, waved good-bye to her classmates and teacher, and looked for her mother. She hid the feelings that were brewing inside her from her teacher. The moment Charlotte saw her mom, though, she threw her bag and lunch container on the ground and burst into tears. Jane held Charlotte's younger sister on her hip while she tried to placate her older child. Jane was exhausted and her patience was wearing thin. She recognized Charlotte was upset and needed comfort, but she was also tired of Charlotte's behavior. Jane, embarrassed by Charlotte's tantrum, guided her screaming daughter out of the school building to the parking lot. Once they were in the car, Jane began to yell. When she raised her voice, Charlotte wailed, and soon her little sister started wailing too.

I ran into Jane the next day at school. She pulled me aside to tell me about her struggles with Charlotte and her parenting stress. She hoped I might have suggestions for how to help. "The moment Charlotte acts out, it's as if a bolt of lightning hits me. I become so charged, it takes my breath away. I lose my cool immediately. The biggest problem is that I have no idea what Charlotte wants, and she won't tell me. I feel so ashamed. What am I doing wrong? What's wrong with Charlotte?"

I listened to Jane and assured her that she was not alone in her parenting stress. Many children hold it together during the school day and reserve their emotional breakdowns for their parents. I confessed that my experience as a parent was similar to hers and that I, too, criticized myself with an inner voice that was often cruel and relentless. I shared a practice that saved my relationship between my children and myself—the practice of *mindfulness* and mindful meditation.

Mindfulness is the practice of intentionally paying attention to the present moment without judgment. By cultivating it, you can be less reactive and more present in your experiences. The MIND framework begins with mindfulness because it is a practice that promotes self-awareness that leads to greater self-regulation—two key skills for social-emotional intelligence.

Being mindful is a skill, and like any skill, it takes practice. Even with practice, this special kind of awareness develops little by little over time. Though mindfulness can be practiced anytime, anywhere, to live and parent more mindfully, it's powerful to start with mindful meditation. You simply pay close attention to your thoughts, feelings, physical sensations, and breath, without judging the experience. Being in a mindful state allows you to pay attention to yourself with curiosity, asking such questions as:

- *What do I need to be aware of at this moment?*

- *What am I feeling or thinking?*

- *Are the physical sensations I'm experiencing connected to a thought or an emotion?*

Paying attention to, and asking about, what is happening allows you to be present in the moment. You will notice how quickly thoughts and emotions come and go and that it's when you get caught up by them—stuck in a thought loop that can cause anxiety, anger, sadness, and other emotions—that they stick around and make you feel uncertain or insecure. As I established my own mindful meditation practice, when I first sat down to meditate, all I heard was my critical inner voice. It would tell me, for example, to make more nutritious meals for my family. I did my best to just listen and not judge what I'd prepared for dinner last night.

Practicing the skill of mindful meditation will make you a more mindful parent. Taking time to learn how to observe your thoughts and feelings without immediately reacting to them makes a big difference when you are parenting. For me, I noticed that I was able to accept my children's actions. I saw what they were doing as a result of what was occurring in their mind and body. I became more patient and curious about the cause of their responses rather than immediately reacting by trying to fix the problem and becoming frustrated by their actions. Over time, I discovered the beauty of mindful awareness: It didn't judge. It just was. It had no opinion; it didn't compare, blame, or shame.

When you apply this mindset to parenting your child, otherwise overwhelming experiences become much less stressful. To get into the mindset of your child, it is best to be as emotionally calm as possible. This stable state allows you to concentrate and ask, "I wonder why my child is doing this?" It is much easier to look at the world the way your child does when you approach their actions and responses (as well as your own) with curiosity and equanimity.

With more awareness of what is happening in the present moment, you can shift your attention to the relationship you have with your child and with yourself as a parent. You will also discover the power of pausing before reacting. Taking a breath can give you the necessary time and perspective to appropriately address your child's needs. But no matter how well intentioned you are as a parent, it can still be very hard at times to be mindful. When you are distracted—angry, sad, frustrated, anxious—it can be difficult to be present in the moment. Don't be hard on yourself.

As you learn the skills of mindfulness and mindful meditation, you can share them with your child. It is helpful to ensure that you feel comfortable with mindfulness practices yourself before introducing them to your child. This practice gives you and your child time together to focus on such skills as self-awareness, self-management, and listening. Let's begin with your own practice. Then we'll move on to practicing with your child.

## Becoming a Mindful Parent

When I became a mother, I felt a constant tension in my body and an underlying sense of anxiety. There were butterflies in my stomach, and I often felt queasy. I questioned my parenting choices and had a nagging inner voice telling me that I wasn't doing things right. There were days when I was tense and angry, but I told myself I had no time (or right) to feel that way. My life was good, and my children were healthy and happy. What was wrong with me? I should just be grateful.

At the time, I lived in Beijing, China. During a very low moment, I confided in a close friend what I was experiencing. I had been feeling out of sorts for many months, but I was reluctant to tell the other mothers I was friendly with because they all appeared to parent in stride. It turns out, I was wrong. When I finally confided in my girlfriend, she told me that she felt the same way. She urged me to meet Dr. Zhou, a traditional Chinese doctor who put meditation and mindfulness at the core of his practice. "He helped me become easier on myself, and now I don't feel so drained when I'm with my children. I can actually enjoy being with them. All I need is ten minutes, more or less, to do mindful meditation. It's changing my relationships. I have so much more patience now."

What did I have to lose? I called Dr. Zhou and arranged to meet him. Dr. Zhou told me that he had to be extra vigilant with his meditation practice when he became a father. He often found himself losing his patience with his daughter and saying all sorts of things that he regretted. Even a master meditation teacher found parenting stressful! I asked him how this would help with my parenting. He told me that I needed to learn to observe my thoughts and feelings and notice the times when they are connected to my parenting. The sections that follow are largely based on the instructions Dr. Zhou passed on to me during a personal conversation with him in 2008. Later, we'll go over some other mindfulness hacks if you initially feel uncertain about any type of meditation.

# How to Practice Mindful Meditation

We'll start with the process of seated meditation, but if you prefer to meditate while moving, there are ways to do this that you can easily research online. Whether seated, upright, lying down, or moving, the principles are the same.

1.  Find a comfortable upright position (sitting on a chair, a sofa, or the floor). There is no need to be uncomfortable.

2.  Determine how long you would like to meditate and set a timer. Five to ten minutes is a good length to start. Close your eyes and sit quietly.

3.  Listen to the sounds around you and pay close attention to them. Focus on the qualities of the sounds, such as the length, pitch, and timing between noises.

4.  Shift your awareness to your body to see if you are holding tension anywhere. Obvious places to mentally scan are

your jaw, shoulders, hands, neck, and forehead between your eyes. Try to release any tension you feel in those places. Notice what it feels like the moment you let the tension go. Observe how you feel when you are not holding tension. Tension might return; notice when it does and release it. Keep observing the coming and going of tension or other physical sensations in your body, as well as monitoring any changes in your emotions.

5. Next, take five to ten breath cycles. Inhale and exhale to complete a cycle. Count each cycle. Notice the subtle differences between each cycle. For instance, your inhale might be longer than your exhale or vice versa.

6. Once you have completed the breath cycles, stop counting and notice what is happening. Your mind might wander; this is normal. Observe, with curiosity, what you are thinking about. Are there thoughts of blame, shame, judgment, or criticism? Are there thoughts about your parenting? Are there thoughts about your child? Pay attention, listen, and observe what is happening inside of you, without judgment. To let go of judgment and get some distance from your personal experiences, it helps to imagine that you are in the audience watching a play of what is going on in your mind. Thoughts will come and go like actors on the stage changing scenes. When the scene changes and a thought passes, return your awareness to your breath. Take a few breath cycles.

7. Eventually, your timer will go off, and when it does, gradually open your eyes and reflect on what you observed.

If you are new to this or if you prefer using guided meditations, there are many good apps available that are helpful in starting a mindfulness meditation practice. To be mindful of your parenting, pay particular attention to the thoughts and feelings you have that relate to you and your child while you are meditating.

I want to share with you what I experienced when I first started meditating because, like many people, I found it quite challenging. At first, I had many waves of thoughts and feelings—anger, frustration, and disappointment—that felt out of control. After a month or so, I began to accept this out-of-control feeling and became better at watching what I was experiencing as opposed to responding to what was happening. I would sit (or walk) and notice my mind always at work—there were always new thoughts, emotions, feelings, and physical sensations. Some days I felt more skilled at meditation, while on other days I felt like a beginner. I started to greet my anger by saying, "Hey, anger, I feel you in my chest. You're hot and tight, aren't you?" The more skillful I became at giving in to what I was experiencing, the less reactive I became as a person. I needed to become less reactive for the sake of my family and myself.

This is all normal. The most important thing to remember is to not judge yourself as a meditator. This is a practice of accepting what is happening right now. For example, maybe you're still feeling angry about the juice your child spilled all over the floor. Accept that you feel angry. Take note of what happens when you meet and greet the anger with acceptance versus resistance. During your practice sessions, it is inevitable that you will experience an unwanted thought or emotion about your parenting or your child. The mind will throw all sorts of thoughts at you—some that you will like and some that are painful. With more awareness and skillful practice, you will learn to choose the thoughts you want to hold on to and discard the unwanted inner chatter by kindly saying to yourself, "I hear you, but this thought is not helping me now."

As Dr. Zhou said, "When you meditate, commit to the moment, commit to being alert, attentive, and ardent. In other words, pay attention and remain aware of what you're doing. Focus on what is happening to you from moment to moment. Pay particular attention to the thoughts you have on parenting and about your child. Notice the stories you tell yourself when you're comparing yourself or your child to others. When you let go of these comparisons and judgments, notice what happens. You will feel at ease with yourself and you can be at ease with your child." His confidence is reassuring.

## Making Time for Mindful Meditation

Many parents have told me they don't have time to meditate. I've heard a whole range of reasons, from "I can't sit still" to "I can't do it because I can't turn off my thoughts." Knowing that you are having thoughts is the start of the process! Watching and observing your inner world come and go without judgment is a skill that takes time to learn.

To get into the habit of meditating, set a short amount of time aside each day, just five or ten minutes to start. If making time to practice every day seems like too much, start with a goal of meditating three to four times a week instead. Be prepared for your meditation time to be interrupted by unexpected events, like your child waking up earlier than usual or your cat getting sick. If meditating while moving is more appealing or realistic for you, you can practice mindful meditation while doing a daily chore or routine, such as cooking, folding the clothes, or walking the dog. Because you will be doing something instead of sitting still, it's easy to become distracted by your surroundings and forget to pay attention to your breath. When that happens, just focus on the action that you are doing, turning the dreaded task of washing dishes, for example, into something you can eagerly anticipate.

Here's how: Focus your attention on every step of the dishwashing process. Call out your actions while washing plates, pots, and pans.

When you squirt soap onto the sponge, say to yourself, "Squirting soap," and when the sponge moves over the dirty plate, say, "Wiping a plate." Calling out your moment-to-moment actions keeps the mind from wandering. As you clean, move your attention to your breath. When you catch your mind wandering, take note of the thought and then redirect your attention to a sensation, such as the water hitting your hands.

Once you start to notice that you are emotionally calmer and able to observe your thoughts and feelings about your parenting or your child's behavior without immediately reacting, it can be very helpful to introduce mindful meditation to your child.

## Introducing Mindfulness and Mindful Meditation to Your Child

Al, the father of one of my students, wondered if he could meditate with his children after being introduced to mindfulness meditation at work. Al and his team met weekly with a mindfulness meditation teacher who facilitated guided meditations and provided instruction on establishing a meditation practice at home. After about a month, Al sensed a physical change in his body and felt less nervous. He brought this more positive energy home and noticed that his children wanted to spend more time with him. "You're fun now, Daddy!" they would say. And surprisingly, Al felt more fun. He wanted to teach his 5- and 7-year-old children about mindfulness meditation, but he was unsure how young children meditated. Would they sit still and know how to monitor their breath? How could he explain it in a child-friendly way? I assured Al that young children can learn mindfulness meditation, but there were some important things to keep in mind.

Your child is developing an awareness of their mental states, such as thoughts and feelings. Mindfulness meditation practice is different for young children. Think of it as uncharted land; it's the beginning of an expedition inward to observe their internal landscape. As we discussed in chapter 1, part of children's developing ToM is having an awareness of their own mental states, as well as an understanding that the mental states of others may differ (and drive other people's actions).

Mindfulness will not change who your child is, but over time, their reactions to experiences will likely change, and so will yours. Whereas we all have emotional moments, you might notice that your child is running less "on automatic" and is more aware of what they are doing. For example, you might notice that instead of bursting into tears when the block tower falls over (a habitual and automatic response), they may pause, assess the situation, and rebuild the tower with a new plan. You might also notice that they stay with a task longer, even when they hit a bump in the road. There may still be times when your child will burst into tears when their tower falls because, even if they were calm and focused, they just need to show their disappointment when it topples over.

Young children need your guidance to get started; they cannot do this alone. I have heard many frustrated parents of young children say, "I told my child about mindfulness. I told them to take a deep breath when they were angry, but it didn't help." If you want your child to use mindfulness meditation as a resource, when you begin to practice, you will have to do it with them. Think of it as a "time-in" as opposed to a time-out.

Your child might wriggle and wiggle during your quiet time together. This is normal. There is no need for you to feel as if you have to control your child's behavior during this time. Instead, focus on *your* mindfulness meditation. Model the practice and enjoy the shared time together. You might even notice that when your child doesn't get a reaction from you, they stop what they are doing and settle into stillness.

Al was nervous about getting started. "I don't want to mess this up!" he said. "Tell me exactly what I *shouldn't* do." I thought Al's request was an interesting way of giving instructions, but I did what he asked.

Here's a list of things *not* to do when practicing mindfulness meditation with your child:

- It is *not* a time to focus on reducing behavior that you would like your child to stop doing (like throwing food on the floor).

- It is *not* a time to coerce your child into feeling a particular way. Allow your child to discover their inner world in their own way. Your job is to provide direction, boundaries, and consistency on how to practice mindfulness meditation.

- It is *not* a time for you to tell your child how to think and feel. It is a time for you and your child to discover how their thoughts and beliefs drive actions and changes. It will take time for your child to grasp the concept of awareness. You'll know your child is starting to understand awareness when they talk more about their feelings and become less reactive.

When you talk to 4- to 8-year-olds about mindfulness and mindfulness meditation, it's good to compare opposites because children can often understand extremes better than subtleties. For example, explain that you are *mindful* when you pause to consider what you are thinking before doing something and *forgetful* when you act without stopping to think. For many people, the word "forgetful" refers to not remembering something, but in this case, children notice that they didn't remember to stop between feeling and responding. Here are a handful of other age-appropriate ideas to share with preschool and early elementary children about mindfulness:

- Some experiences make us feel hot (angry, jealous, jumpy), while others make us feel cool (peaceful, calm, loose).

- Like the weather, our feelings are constantly changing. One moment we can feel stormy, like when we are angry, and the next moment we can feel sunny, like when we are happy.

- Mindfulness meditation is a time to become friends with yourself. We make friends with ourselves in the same way we make friends with others, by learning about them and showing them kindness and respect. We should also remember to treat ourselves the same way we treat others—with care.

- To be a good friend to yourself, it's important to be aware of what you are doing, to listen to what you say to yourself, and to pay attention to how you are feeling, from moment to moment. You can be a detective looking for connections between your thoughts, feelings, and actions—for example, by questioning whether a thought made you act in a certain way.

Think about your daily routine and try to find a time when you can devote ten minutes to mindfulness with your child. Many parents take ten minutes at bedtime. It helps to be consistent with the schedule. You won't be asking your child to sit quietly for ten minutes. Ten minutes is all that's needed for the entire experience—to prepare, to sit quietly, and to reflect together. Go easy on yourself. Begin by committing to at least once a week, with a goal of building up to three to four times a week.

When introducing your child to the practice, gently guide them by drawing from your own experience with mindful meditation. Some children like to practice mindfulness with their "lovey" (a favorite toy, stuffed animal, blanket, or other object that makes them feel secure). And use a timer (on your phone or a portable baking timer) so your child knows how long the experience will take.

Here is a sample script you can follow that has proven successful in the classroom, but of course you're encouraged to use words that you think will work best for you and your child.

I'm going to meditate with you now. Let's sit in a comfortable position. It's time to put our mindfulness HAT on. (*Pantomime putting a hat on your head. Young children, in particular, find this fun.*) The H-A-T reminds us of important things:

H is for "happening": Let's pay attention to what is *happening* inside of us while we are sitting still. Notice sensations in your body—for instance, a tingle from excitement or a tightness from anger.

A is for "allow": While we sit, *allow* whatever is happening to just happen. Sit quietly and accept how you are feeling right now. Accept and allow the wave of excitement to pass through you if you are thinking about ice cream, for example.

T is for "time": Give yourself quiet *time* to notice your thoughts and feelings come and go without reacting to them. Pay attention to what you say to yourself. Do your words make you feel a certain way? Notice whether you're kind or unkind to yourself.

Okay, our HAT is on and we are ready to start. I'll set the timer for X minutes (*three to five is usually a good starting point*). Close your eyes or look down. (*If your child feels uncomfortable closing their eyes, ask them to choose what they would like to look at—for example, a picture in their room or a spot on the floor.*)

First, let's release the tension, or any tight feeling, in our bodies. Make a fist and squeeze as hard as you can. Then open your hand and feel the tension or tightness leave. Now let's release the tension in our shoulders. Squeeze them together and then drop your shoulders down. Notice the tension release. Let's do the face now. Scrunch your face and then relax it. Keep scanning other parts of your body. (*Tensing and relaxing are opposite sensations, and it's easy for children to feel the difference. These instructions help them become familiar with the connection between physical sensations and emotions.*)

Next, let's breathe in and out together. Breathe. Let's do this together five times. (*Count together. Follow your child's breath. No need to tell them to breathe in a certain way—remember, it's not a time to focus on behavior.*)

Now we will keep paying attention to our breath. Your attention might wander to a thought or story about something that happened in the past or something you want to happen in the future. Maybe you can watch the story like you watch YouTube or TV. Try to listen to the story and notice whether it makes you feel a certain way. (*This is a good point to check your child's body for any tension, similar to the squeezing, and to notice when the story is finished.*) When your story (or thought) is finished, take a breath and listen for any sounds in the room.

I'm going to stop talking now and want to just sit here with you. (*Every now and then, check in with your child and remind them that you are nearby, breathing and being dragged off by waves of stories, tension, and feelings too.*)

Although these instructions are useful, you might still want some additional guidance to get started. If so, you can search for a few mindfulness apps for children and listen to the instructions with your child without a screen. The screen can distract your child from the experience of moving inward.

Children actually enjoy mindfulness meditation—taking time out to pay attention to what is happening to them, in the moment, especially when they are not being forced to take a time-out for their behavior. We often tell our children to take a time-out when their behavior is more than we can tolerate and they need to cool down, but seldom do we give children time to check in with their inner world when they are feeling calm and at ease.

Children are intrigued when they can see (the images in their head), hear, and feel the world inside of them in the same way they can tune in to the world around them. Children seem pleased when they are given the time to sit with themselves and look inward and when the adults in their lives listen wholeheartedly to what they say, without judgment. Here are some comments children have shared:

- Jack (6 years old) talked about his inner voice. "I hear myself talking sometimes, and sometimes I feel sad because I say things that aren't nice. I decided that if I was going to talk to myself, I had to say nice things. I didn't want a hot mind talking to me; it made me mad. I want a cool mind talking to me; it makes me calm."

- Violet (5 years old) explained how memories grab her attention. She could see them (her thoughts) like a movie, but they were in her brain and they stirred up her emotions. "I thought about all the things I did with my grandma before she died. We were apple picking and then went to make a pie. I was happy and sad at the same time; two feelings at once!"

- Carson (5 years old) described being dragged away by thoughts about the future. "I went to Disneyland! I was just sitting here, and I went to Disneyland. It was like I was time traveling!"

- Beth (3 years old) said, "I didn't like sitting still. I didn't like doing that."

Note that at 3 years old, Beth clearly expressed her dislike of the stillness, which is normal for a young preschooler. Over time, however, young children often come to enjoy it with the patient encouragement of their parents to keep at it. If your child has a really hard time sitting still, you can give them an object to hold and squeeze. Interacting with a physical object that a child can feel and manipulate while sitting often alleviates restlessness. Children, like adults, don't need to sit to meditate; they can walk or stand.

# Strengthening Your Parent-Child Bond

After mindfully meditating with your child, take time to share what you experienced. Reflect together by letting your child know that you have an inner world of thoughts and feelings that is shaping what you say and do, just like they do. Practicing mindfulness together not only models self-awareness and self-regulation for your child, but it also fortifies your parent-child bond. This happens when you share your inner worlds with each other, without judgment.

Share what you thought about and how your thoughts connected to your feelings. Then ask your child about their experience and carefully listen to what they say without telling them how to feel or think. Let them share in the way that you shared with them. For example, share a very specific observation with your child, such as, "I thought about how you mixed green and blue together when you painted today. I remembered watching you swirl the paint, and the action made me feel dizzy. The thought made my head feel light. All this happened as I sat quietly with my eyes closed. What happened while you sat quietly?"

Nurturing parents help young children develop a sense of security and love. When you have a consistent and caring relationship with your child, you empower them to become caring people too. This is why your reactions matter and why you want to control them instead of having them control you. When you are more self-aware of your reactions, you will become more mindful of the bond you are creating with your child.

# How Practicing Mindfulness Benefits You and Your Child

The best way to teach your child to be mindful is to embody and model the practice yourself. Your mindful meditation practice can be profoundly beneficial to you[65] and at the same time provide an opportunity to bond with your child and start an early habit of calming the mind, stabilizing your focus, and becoming aware of the moment leading to more acceptance of your parenting style and your child. A growing body of research with children and adolescents supports the benefits of mindfulness training, including greater empathy and perspective-taking skills, reduced stress, and improved prosocial skills.[66] Although there is limited published research on the effects of mindfulness training in preschoolers, experts suggest that teaching mindfulness to young children might be beneficial because of their rapid brain development.[67] In particular, scientists have suggested that self-regulation is surprisingly malleable during the preschool years and that mindfulness can potentially improve it.[68] When young children are guided to repeatedly pause and reflect on their experiences, they strengthen their emotion regulation skills.

After learning about mindfulness meditation, many parents comment on the positive effect it has on their parenting self-esteem and how they've become better at connecting with their child. Jane (from the beginning of the chapter) shared that she felt a significant shift in her relationship with Charlotte after she started a mindful parenting practice. "Now I feel confident giving Charlotte boundaries and guidance because I take my cues from her actions and I give her space to develop her sense of identity, which I see as separate from mine. When I meditate, I witness myself thinking about the parenting process and am much more intentional with my priorities. For the first time, I can say I'm learning to enjoy parenting."

## Growing Together in Mindfulness

Practicing mindfulness meditation with your child may seem like an overwhelming task with few immediate rewards. One important point to remember is that you are practicing this skill *together*. Throughout this ongoing experience, you may discover things about your child—for example, how they pay attention, calm down, and make decisions. You will notice changes if you practice frequently and consistently.

In closing, we offer a handful of key things to consider that may help you get started as you and your child develop a mindful meditation practice. Your role as a parent is to:

- Create a nurturing environment that includes a sense of safety, care, and support

- Guide your child to notice that feelings change; they come and go quickly, like waves in the sea

- Explain that there are no right or wrong feelings; feelings and thoughts should not be judged

- Model how to identify thoughts and name emotions, reminding them that emotions have names: angry, sad, happy (thinking back to chapter 2, remember that talking with your child about feelings helps develop social awareness and emotional intelligence)

- Point out that thoughts and feelings can be connected to physical sensations in the body (like a tight chest or a lump in the throat)

- Tell them how to focus on breathing as a way to slow down a thought or emotion, especially when the feeling is uncomfortable

- Reinforce that everyone has thoughts and feelings but that theirs might differ from those of others; what makes one person happy might make someone else sad (see chapter 1 on theory of mind development for more about children's growing understanding of mental states)

Knowing how to be in a more mindful state is the first part of the MIND framework. The M in MIND represents being mindful, to underscore the importance of self-awareness and self-regulation. Mindfulness teaches us to pause. It creates some space between our feelings and thoughts and our responses to them, space that gives us time to intentionally and skillfully respond to how we're feeling and what we're thinking.

Remember, being mindful is a lifelong practice, and there will always be moments when you are more mindful and others when you respond before pausing. Now that you know how to move into a mindful state, take this skill with you to the next chapter on inquiry. In the next chapter, you will learn to pause to gather information on how your child is reacting and gain new insight into what they are experiencing while considering their age and stage of development.

# CHAPTER 6

# Inquiry Reveals What Your Child Is Feeling

The restaurant called out, "Order ready for Jennifer!"

Rebecca turned to her daughter and said, "That's your hot dog, Jen. Let's go get it." Jenny, 4 years old, and her mom, Rebecca, went to pick it up.

Jenny's eyes widened when she saw her hot dog and french fries. She smiled, then instructed, "Ketchup, Mommy, I want ketchup." Rebecca and Jenny went to the condiment bar to pump ketchup. "I want to do it, Mommy." Using all her force, Jenny pushed down on the pump, and a mound of ketchup landed in the middle of the hot dog and oozed over the sides of the bun. Jenny looked horrified and flopped to the restaurant floor. "Now I can't eat it!" she screamed.

Perplexed and frustrated, Rebecca's chest tightened and she thought, *Really?* Her daughter's behavior was unpredictable, which left Rebecca feeling tense and nervous a lot of the time.

Have you observed your child rapidly shift emotions, like Jenny did? She went from excited to determined to completely miserable all within the span of one minute. Sudden shifts like this likely leave you confused and sometimes exasperated. The MIND framework can help make sense of both your child's actions and your reactions to them as we move from the M for "mindfulness" to the I for "inquiry." In this chapter, you'll inquire about your child's developing mind so that you can guide and model responses that support their emotional development. Once you are in a more mindful state about your parenting, feeling balanced and even-tempered, it's easier to inquire without judgment and see the world through the eyes of your child. You can do this by asking about your child's actions, listening to their response with respect, and being aware of your assumptions about why they do what they do. The questions you ask and the way you ask them will help you and your child bring awareness to their reactions.

When you inquire about both your own and your child's reactions, you're investigating what you experience. You're gathering information about what you are experiencing physically and how these feelings connect to what you are telling yourself. To do all this, you'll want to get curious—to pay attention to what is happening inside of you while your child is having an outburst, without judging either one of you.

Once you are able to gather information on what you and your child are experiencing, you can gain insight from what is happening. To gain insight, when you are feeling calm, reframe how you perceive the situation by imagining the experience through the eyes of your child. Inquiring into *how* and *what* you experience and what you perceive your child is experiencing brings insight to your response.

The more familiar you are with this process, the easier it will be to teach it to your child. You can help your child identify what they are feeling and then notice how these feelings trigger thoughts and actions. Then you can guide your child to consider how their actions might make others feel and help them find effective ways to communicate and collaborate so that everyone feels understood.

## Mindfulness as the Basis for Inquiry

To begin the inquiry process, start with mindfulness. Paying attention to your physical sensations helps you understand whether you are opening up to an experience or closing down. For instance, when you feel relaxed or happy, you are probably more open to what you are experiencing. In contrast, when there is a tightness or tension in your body, it might connect to anger or frustration, and unkind words or harsh actions tend to follow. In this case, you are not ready to gather information about the experience. Wait until you are feeling calm to inquire.

Joseph Goldstein, a well-known Western meditation teacher, talks about the changing nature of feelings. He reminds us that when we pause to let the mind settle, we notice the ever-changing nature of our moods, thoughts, and levels of physical tension. He points out that the state of mind is never static; it bounces from here to there, so it takes work to react with clear intention.[69]

In a reactive state, tension tends to stay trapped in the body, making it difficult to attune to what you are experiencing. When there is tension, once you have identified the feelings that caused it, notice the size. If your feelings are still large and overwhelming, wait until your feelings get smaller. When they are small and manageable, you can focus.

Get curious about how you are perceiving your child's behavior and observe what you tell yourself. As parents, our inner voice can say a range of things that plant doubt, judgment, and fear, like, *I must be a bad parent if my kids behave this way* or *I'm scared that I don't know what I'm doing.* Once your feelings are manageable, ask yourself:

- Are you feeling doubt? Restlessness? Rage?

- How do you really want your child to act?

- Are you okay with their current actions? If not, what needs to change and why do you believe it needs to change?

As you learn to still your mind, you will notice what you are feeling and perceiving with more clarity. Mindfulness helps soften your response to the feelings connected to external systems so that you can remain open to what's happening in the moment. This can also allow you to carefully explore your assumptions about how you think your child should behave and how you believe you should parent compared to what's really happening. Mindfulness makes it easier to attune to what you are experiencing and to inquire about your perceptions with kindness and curiosity.

## Roll with Patience

When you start to inquire about the nature of your child's conflict, you might experience a new range of emotions that throw you off-kilter. After all, the mind is always in flux, with feelings and thoughts constantly shifting your mood, tipping your scale from balanced to unbalanced. Think back to the work of Urie Bronfenbrenner discussed in chapter 4: his research reminds us that there are external systems, both micro (family, friends) and macro (culture, societal norms), that influence you and your child, for better or worse. These systems affect your beliefs, thoughts, and opinions—and might stir up fear and even pain.

When you find yourself becoming unbalanced, it helps to have a mantra. To restore balance, a favorite is: "Roll with patience." These three words serve as a reminder to steady yourself and to just roll with what's emerging. If you can be patient enough to be present during your child's outburst, you will gain information and insight into what your child is experiencing in the moment.

Here's what that looks like in the scenario at the start of the chapter: As Jenny glared at the hot dog bun with ketchup oozing over the sides, she eventually stopped crying. But Rebecca was still in panic mode. Would Jenny start screaming all over again? Tension gripped Rebecca's jaw. She knew she needed to get into mindful mode instead, so she began taking deep breaths as she mentally repeated, *Roll with it, roll with it, patience, roll with patience.* Repeating the mantra reminded her of the ever-changing reality of each moment and the amount of patience required to be a parent.

In this mind space, Rebecca was able to investigate why the incident upset her so much. She realized she was afraid of Jenny's unpredictable behavior—today, in particular, she resented wasting precious time resolving her daughter's outburst when what she really needed to do was clean the house like she planned. When Rebecca acknowledged that she was tense about the loss of time, she felt more at ease, simply by identifying the source of the tension.

The next step after inquiring about the nature of your response is to shift your focus from you to your child, so you can begin to inquire about the source of their conflict. "Conflict" here means any interactive process in which there is a disagreement *within* oneself or *between* oneself and others. Your child's behavior can be caused by a personal conflict with the self (intrapersonal) or by how they are perceiving an event with others (interpersonal) born of opposing opinions, beliefs, and ideas. You've surely observed these types of conflicts, for instance, when your child gets frustrated because they can't draw a perfect circle (intrapersonal conflict) or when your child argues with a friend about who's a faster runner (interpersonal conflict). Because your child's views and actions will accord with their age and stage of development, apply patience and knowledge with these factors in mind to help them understand how to resolve conflict.

In Rebecca's case, once she felt herself calming down, she was able to make this shift by first watching Jenny's actions with curiosity, naming them to herself: *She's looking at the hot dog bun … folding a napkin in her hands … wiping the napkin on the side of the bun to brush the ketchup onto the plate … getting ketchup on her fingers … wondering if she will cry because her fingers are sticky.* Naming Jenny's actions kept Rebecca in the present moment, made her less reactive and more aware of what Jenny was doing, and kept her from judging her feelings and her daughter's actions. So what was her daughter likely feeling? Rebecca next asked herself. She knew that Jenny liked things to be orderly, so the messy blob of ketchup no doubt upset and unbalanced her. Later, when they were home and Jenny was calm, Rebecca resolved, she would ask Jenny about the source of the conflict (see below).

It might seem like all of this takes a lot of time—for you to first inquire about your state of mind during any given incident and then inquire about your child's—but it really takes only moments in your mind and gets easier and easier with practice.

## Helping Your Child Become an Inquirer

Once you use inquiry to gather information about conflicts and you are able to understand what your child is experiencing without negatively reacting, you are ready to teach your child to be an inquirer. The objective is to help your child become curious about their intra- and interpersonal conflicts and to consider how best to react to them. Ultimately, over time and with development, you'll guide your child to pause between stimulus and response so they can choose actions that are thoughtful and intentional.

Teaching your child to be an inquirer has many benefits. Inquiry broadens children's development in numerous ways and helps them to:[70,71,72]

- Notice more details about their experience

- Generate and develop ideas

- Communicate and collaborate with others

- Increase their ability to solve problems

The good news is that your child is already a natural inquirer. You may have noticed that your young child asks an endless stream of questions: "Why is the sky blue?" "Where does milk come from?" In fact, research investigating naturalistic conversations of preschoolers with adults found that children ask around seventy-six information-seeking questions per hour![73]

By asking your child about their experience instead of telling them your interpretation of it, you are actively engaging your child in constructing their own understanding of the world. Inquiry can help you better understand your child's point of view. As you listen to them, you can share your views too. The ultimate goal is for these open discussions to help support your child's social and emotional development.

Remember that the ability to think about the thinking of others is developmental, so you will need to "roll with patience," giving your child time and offering guidance on how to do this. Take a moment to review what you know about the development of theory of mind, using figure 1 in chapter 1 as a reminder of how mental state understanding grows and changes across development:

- Young children notice that people have different desires, likes, and dislikes, on which they act.

- In the preschool years, children learn that people have beliefs that can be false. As your child gets older, they recognize that some of their mental states, such as fear and jealousy, can be hidden from others.

- As they enter the formal school years, children gain an understanding of the stream of consciousness—that the mind is constantly full of thoughts.

Recalling the research in part one can help you modify expectations of your child, recognizing that it take times for them to acquire a deeper understanding of emotional intelligence. Nevertheless, it is surprising how well young children can identify their feelings and how creative they are when describing what they are experiencing. Consider 3-year-old Lamar flapping his arms, hopping up and down, and saying, "I'm all jumpy like a frog—my arms and legs want to move like this" or 5-year-old Wadeya pointing to her forehead and sharing, "I've got two feelings. There's some electricity in my stomach and a few moths in my head, right here."

# Inquiring with a Feelings Jar

Chapter 2 offered some strategies to expand your child's emotional vocabulary through picture books. Building on these techniques, what follows are directions for making a *feelings jar*—a tool that helps children inquire about their inner experiences and helps parents gather information and gain insight about their children's feelings. A feelings jar can be made with your child as soon as they are able to identify and talk about emotions.

---

**Objective:** To demonstrate to your child that feelings and thoughts are not permanent, good or bad, but rather, a source of information. Being well informed on what's passing through the body and the mind, in the moment, helps people make wise decisions.

## Teaching points:

- Feelings come and go, and they tell us something.

- Feelings range in intensity—they can be big or small.

- More than one feeling can be felt at the same time.

## Materials:

- Label for the jar

- Crayons or markers

- Clear jar to hold the pom-poms

- Colored pom-poms, in sets of two of the same color, one big and one small for each of the following colors: yellow, white, green, blue, purple, red, orange, black, pink, and brown

## Directions:

1. Ask your child to decorate the label with crayons or markers and write *Feelings Jar* on it (or write it for them if they can't write yet). Stick the label on the jar.

2. Explain that each pair of same-colored pom-poms represents a particular feeling (happy, sad, excited) and that they come in different sizes because feelings can be big or small. (Pom-poms are used here because they are physical objects that readily represent abstract concepts, like feelings. Using a tangible object to represent an intangible idea aids children's comprehension.)

3. Line up the colored pom-poms by color (still in sets of big and small), then ask your child to assign a feeling to each color, for example, green for anxiety, black for fear, purple for jealousy, pink for excited, and so on. Younger children will likely need guidance to name emotions beyond happy, sad, angry, and scared.

---

To get started using the feelings jar as part of your regular routine, pick a time when you and your child are feeling calm, like right before their bedtime story, to use the jar as a tool to reflect on and add closure to their day. As children get older (4+ years) and are familiar with how to use the jar, pull it out after outbursts to help them process their feelings and devise ways to take alternative actions in the future.

You can use the following script as a guide, but as always, feel free to customize it with examples specific to their experiences and scenarios they can easily relate to. You can begin by retelling a part of your day, using the pom-poms to represent the size of your feelings.

Today when I talked with Aunt Sue, I felt very happy (*pull out the large yellow pom-pom and place it in front of you*). While I was talking with her, Lenny chewed on my shoe and I became angry (*pull out the large red pom-pom*), but when I told Lenny to drop the shoe, he listened and my anger became smaller (*switch out the large red pom-pom for the small one*). Aunt Sue asked me why I yelled at Lenny, and I told her about the shoe. She said training a puppy was a lot of work. After Aunt Sue talked about Lenny, my feelings changed. I was still happy, but the feeling was smaller (*change the big yellow pom-pom for the little one*). I also felt sad (*pull out the small blue pom-pom*) and tired when I thought about how much we still need to teach Lenny. (*Looking at the pom-poms, explain how you felt two feelings at the same time and how some feelings change from big to small.*)

Then ask your child to recount something from their own day, expressing their feelings about it the same way you did.

Using the feelings jar after your child has had an emotional outburst can help them become more aware of the cause and effect of their actions. Once you and your child are feeling calm and are able to talk about the experience, pull out the feelings jar and inquire about what just happened. The example below revisits the story from the beginning of the chapter about Rebecca and Jenny. Notice how Rebecca *does not* tell Jenny how she was feeling. Instead, she uses the feelings jar to *ask* Jenny about her feelings and to consider her actions.

*Rebecca:*  Today you cried when there was too much ketchup on the hot dog bun. Let's try taking the pom-poms out of the jar to show all of your feelings at that time.

*Jenny:*  I was angry (*big red pom-pom*) and hungry (*no pom-pom for that feeling!*) and afraid (*big black pom-pom*).

*Rebecca:*  Oh, a big afraid?

*Jenny:*  It wasn't a big feeling. It was a small one. (*Swap the big pom-pom for the small one.*)

*Rebecca:*  Do you remember what made you afraid?

*Jenny:*  I was mad that I wouldn't be able to eat my hot dog because it was too messy, and I was so hungry. I didn't know what would happen to all that ketchup—I just wanted a little bit of it in a straight line, and the huge blob scared me.

Rebecca: (Thinking: *Jenny was afraid of the ketchup? Her tears were from fear? While I was frustrated and worried about losing time, she was afraid.*) Thanks for sharing your feelings with me. From your tears at the restaurant, I saw that you had some big and small feelings. I'm glad to know more about them now.

This example shows how using a feelings jar helps a parent gather valuable information about their child's feelings so they can respond without judgment and make their child feel safe and accepted.

## Gathering Insight into Your Child's Feelings

As you inquire about your child's feelings, you might start to see some common themes emerging as to the nature of their conflicts. Recall that conflict is an interactive process in which there is a disagreement *within* oneself or *between* oneself and others. To identify sources of conflict, you need to listen to your child very carefully. Listening requires turning off your inner chatter (the voice in your head that is always talking to you) and watching and listening to what your child says and does. Inner chatter can be very distracting, so you will need to be mindful of when it's happening, gently instructing your inner voice to be quiet.

When you still your thoughts, recognize that something has caused your child to react in a certain way. Now that you are relaxed and observant, aim to stay warm, attuned, and responsive to their experience to determine the source of conflict and to plan a wise response. As you listen to and observe your child, remember that conflict is deeply connected to one's awareness of a situation. The more familiar you and your child are with identifying feelings and thoughts, the more comfortable they will be sharing them.

Conflicts can alter children's (and adults') moods and behavior. It is natural to experience conflict; it can't be avoided. Your goal is to help your child identify conflict and learn how to manage it. Raising a socially and emotionally intelligent child who is well equipped to appropriately manage conflict requires guiding them to understand whether the conflict is *within* the self or *between* the self and others. In doing so, you are helping your child:

- Recognize the difference between what they were hoping would happen and what actually happened

- Relate to others when they have incompatible wishes or different viewpoints

Keep in mind that your child might not be able to tell you what's causing the conflict or that it might be unrelated to what's happening at the moment. For instance, they might stop eating their favorite vegetable because their friend told them that eating too many carrots will turn you into a bumblebee. Trying to identify the conflict helps validate your child's experience. When you co-create strategies to manage conflict with your child, you are simultaneously enhancing several developing social-emotional skills, such as resilience, collaboration, and self-awareness.

## Helping Your Child Manage *Within* Conflicts

One common source of a child's conflict is a discrepancy between their desire and the actual outcome. For example, when children want to play a new game but can't follow the instructions on their own, they may experience an internal conflict. These conflicts, for children, occur when expectations don't match reality, or what my 6-year-old students used to refer to as a "mismatch." Mismatches can occur when a child's skill ability—such as problem solving, fine motor skills (hand maneuvers used for tasks like writing and cutting with scissors), or gross motor skills (coordinated large body movements needed to climb a tree)—isn't at the level they would like it to be.

To help your child manage their frustration when mismatches occur, revisit the "Planning and Reflecting with Your Child" section in chapter 3, as the technique outlined there supports children in anticipating and reflecting on conflicts within the self. As a reminder, here are a few things you can do with your child to nurture planning and reflecting:

- Check in with your child in between routines (morning, meals, and bedtime) by talking about their plans, experiences, and reflections

- Ask your child about what they will do next and the anticipated outcome

- Troubleshoot together before beginning a plan and clearly define boundaries

- Reflect on the outcome together by discussing what worked well and what changes can be made in the future

As your child gets older, identifying internal conflicts can become more difficult. The ToM continuum shows us that starting in the later preschool years, children understand that they can hide their feelings from others. Recall Henry and his mother from chapter 2: Henry suddenly became very quiet when he turned 5. He no longer talked out loud, his frustration was more controlled, and his mother had no idea what he was thinking about—Henry could now hide his thoughts and feelings from others. She was unaware when he was having a conflict within, struggling with his thoughts. When he tried something new and the outcome didn't match what he imagined, for instance, Henry told himself he was stupid. The more his mother listened and observed him, the more sure she was that something wasn't right. She started asking Henry more questions and focused on being responsive to his needs and validating what he experienced. She made it explicit that she, too, had an inner voice, like everyone does, and that, at times, that voice could be quite unkind. Henry was relieved to learn that his parent also experienced conflicts within and that this was common to most people. Henry didn't feel so alone.

Help your child understand that, like Henry, they, too, have an inner critic, or what my 6-year-old students labeled their "hot mind"—the critical inner voice that judges what they do and compares them to others. And it's this hot mind that makes them react without stopping to think about the consequences of their actions. When Julia (5 years old) realized that her inner voice was her talking to herself, she said, "Well, that's just silly. I shouldn't say mean things to me. I should be kind to me."

When your child is experiencing a conflict from within, inquire about what they are saying to themselves and remember Julia's sage advice that people should be kind to themselves. Here are some questions to ask your child:

- What are you telling yourself? What is your inner voice saying right now? Take a break and listen to your own thoughts.

- Do you have to believe what you tell yourself?

- How do you feel when you tell yourself that? Are you being kind to yourself? Or does what you say to yourself make you feel sad, angry, or frustrated?

- Would you say what you said to yourself to a friend? Pick one of your friends and imagine saying to them what you said to yourself. Does it feel right to talk to them, or to yourself, this way?

- What helps cool down your mind when it is too hot?

- What is an idea you have to help solve this problem? Let's make a plan to try that together next time!

# Helping Your Child Manage *Between* Conflicts

Conflicts between self and others can occur when your thinking is not flexible and when your point of view is considered to be the only one that matters. You want your child to know:

- That everyone has their own point of view, which needs to be respected

- How to respond when their view is not being accepted by others

- How someone might respond when their view is rejected

Organizational psychologists recognize that a high level of social and emotional intelligence makes for a good team player. Strong team players can bring their own knowledge and creativity to the table while at the same time respecting and appreciating the viewpoints of others.[74] Importantly, you want your child to share ideas instead of stifling them, to show humility and celebrate others. In essence, you want them to recognize the need to balance the importance of the group and the importance of the individual. To do this, your child needs to understand that positive relationships require considering what they believe and recognizing and accepting that the beliefs of others may differ from their own.

This example illustrates how to use the feelings jar to imagine the perspective of another person and compare points of view. After comparing the differences, you can guide your child to think through a resolution.

Parent:   I heard you arguing with Esther. Can you please show me all the feelings you can recall from the argument?

Child:   (Pulls out the big red pom-pom.)

Parent:   Any other feelings?

*Child:*     No, I was just angry.

*Parent:*     How do you think Esther felt?

*Child:*     (Points to the big red pom-pom and pulls out the small yellow pom-pom as well.)

*Parent:*     Esther felt a little happy, too? What made Esther happy?

*Child:*     Esther always wins, and I wanted to win today.

*Parent:*     So you think Esther had two feelings and you had one? If you could tell Esther something, what would you want her to know?

*Child:*     I'd tell her I want to win too.

*Parent:*     And what if you won? How would you feel? And what about Esther—how would she feel?

*Child:*     Me (pulls out the big yellow pom-pom) and Esther (points to the small blue one).

*Parent:*     You'd feel really happy if you won, and Esther would be a little sad. And how would you react to Esther?

*Child:*     (Pausing to think) I'd say, "Nice try."

*Parent:*     That's kind of you. You'd make Esther feel okay even if she lost.

*Child:*     Yeah.

Notice that the parent did not tell the child how to feel or suggest how the other child felt. They just asked questions and listened to their child's responses. When you do this, your child learns that there is no right or wrong feeling that they should experience and that they can only imagine how someone else is feeling.

Furthermore, note that the child chose to resolve the conflict in the way they would have liked to be treated. It's important to hear how your child would resolve their conflict. Help your child understand that others might not resolve things in the same way, which will stir up feelings they'll then have to manage. You can mention to your child that, at times, they will need to "roll with patience" when navigating conflicts with others.

Inquiry requires pausing to gather information on how your child is reacting and gaining insight into what they are experiencing in the moment, considering their age and stage of development. Remind yourself to be patient when you notice a change in mood. When you are feeling calm, return to asking questions about what your child is doing and investigate how you are responding. Gather information and gain insight about what you experience, how you react, and what you perceive your child is experiencing. As you inquire, you might discover that you are defaulting to shame or blame and being critical of yourself or your child. The next chapter will look at how to be less judgmental of yourself and your child as we proceed to the next element of the MIND framework: N for "nonjudgment."

# CHAPTER 7

# Nonjudgmentally Observe to Understand Your Child

Brittney came running to her mom, Audrey. Audrey scooped her 2-year-old daughter into her arms. "Hi, sweet pea. Mommy is so happy to see you." Brittney's smile faded as her eyes darted toward her teacher. She lowered them as the teacher walked their way. "Hi, Mrs. England," Mrs. Howe said. Audrey smiled and nodded. She tried to ignore the tightness in her chest. Whenever Mrs. Howe initiated the conversation, she knew Brittney had been up to no good.

"Brittney's had some trouble sharing this week. Today in the schoolyard, she hoarded the sand toys," said Mrs. Howe.

Audrey listened while Brittney hid her face on her mother's shoulder. Mrs. Howe continued, "This afternoon, Brittney took a bucket from her friend and then threw sand at her. When we asked Brittney to share, she screamed, 'It's mine!' Please have a talk with her about sharing, and we'll do the same."

"Yes, sure," Audrey responded. The word "hoarded" angered her. Audrey felt she needed to defend her daughter. "Brittney's a really good sharer at home. I'll be sure to remind her to share with her friends at school."

As Audrey turned to leave, a few parents whispered to one another. Were they talking about Brittney? Or Audrey's parenting? Audrey smiled at them with the tight feeling still in her chest. On the drive home, her mind swirled with judgment. *What's wrong with Brittney?*

*Have I raised a monster?* (shame). *No, she shares at home, it must be the school* (blame). *Maybe the school is teaching this selfish behavior and they don't even realize it* (criticism). By the time Audrey turned into their driveway, she was upset and drained.

When you feel confused by your child's actions, your first reaction may be to wrongfully judge your child or yourself for their behavior, defaulting to shame, blame, and criticism. Judging others can be good or bad. The term "judgment" is used in this chapter to refer to perceiving your child's actions and your own through a negative lens.

Audrey may have been less judgmental about Brittney's "it's mine" behavior if she knew more about theory of mind development in toddlers and preschoolers. If she knew, more specifically, that toddlers are just beginning to develop the ability to take the perspective of others, which makes sharing challenging. Researchers have examined the development of sharing in young children as a window onto early pro-social, or kindhearted, behaviors (helping, cooperating, and comforting). The good news is that as toddlers approach their second birthday, sharing becomes more frequent with less need for support and encouragement from peers or adults.[75] Interestingly, one study found that toddlers who used more ownership language ("mine," "yours") were more likely to share with same-age peers.[76] That is, children's understanding of ownership—which things belong to them versus others—is an important factor in children's propensity to share.[77]

Putting child development knowledge to the side for a moment, take a look at shades of judgment, such as shame (the painful feeling of humiliation), blame (feeling that someone or something else is at fault), and criticism (expressing disapproval of someone or something) and what judgment does to your relationship with your child. It clouded Audrey's mind and her thoughts about Brittney, which influenced both her parenting and how she reflected on the conversation with Brittney's teacher.

Audrey noticed that her judgment lingered. She was in a bad mood when she got home, and those negative feelings affected how she responded to Brittney. Brittney asked for an apple for a snack, and instead of giving it to her, Audrey said, "Today it's carrot sticks or nothing." Audrey thought, *I'm not going to reward Brittney with what she wants when she can't share.* Does this happen to you too?

Bring to mind a time when you have experienced this. As you reflect, be as honest as possible and notice whether you feel a little vulnerable. This is normal. Judgment is like a tornado—everyone gets tussled by the high winds. This gets us back to the third component of the MIND framework. As this chapter focuses on nonjudgment, you will learn how to place less judgment on your child's behavior and your parenting through a process of observing and accepting your child's *emotional approach*—their personal style for responding to relationships and experiences—and identifying both of your needs.

To start, cultivate a state of nonjudgment by thinking about the developmental continuums we talked about in part one of this book. Recall that it is likely that not until preschool will your child begin to understand how to take the perspective of others. And they do not start understanding the concept of stream of consciousness until the early grade school years. Other abilities, such as executive function, with skills like self-awareness and self-regulation, are also developing rapidly in the preschool and grade school years. Are you judging your child for behavior that is typical of their developmental stage? Before you judge your child's behavior, remember that there are many actions that might seem personal but are common in children of a particular age range.

Respecting your child's development and their approach to experiences rather than trying to control their reactions models nonjudgment. Let's consider your child's emotional approach.

## Observing Your Child's Social and Emotional Approach

Your child's response to relationships and experiences is not static and changes depending on their development and a number of internal and external factors. Keep in mind that your child's emotional approach—the intensity with which they respond to experiences—might be radically different from yours and will evolve as they develop. For example, your child might be reserved in new environments while you feel comfortable in them. We've chosen to highlight this topic because we know that children are going through a great deal of social-emotional development and we can help them build these skills to foster emotional intelligence.

In my classroom, I would continually remind my students to be aware of certain social and emotional approaches, including how to think about another's point of view, ways to join a group that make classmates respond well, and self-regulation techniques. Neuroscientist Richard Davidson describes different social and emotional styles and highlights that happiness and wellness come from self-awareness, self-regulation, adaptability, and resilience.[78] Davidson stresses paying attention to what we do and say in changing contexts, without judgment. I was eager to reinforce these skills with my 4- to 6-year-old students because they were just starting to develop an awareness of their own emotional approach. What a perfect time to get them to start thinking about their thoughts, feelings, and actions!

I remembered what I'd learned from Kim's mom, Saeri (in chapter 2), who taught her daughter to read her classmates' body language. She taught me to reinforce social and emotional skills by explicitly informing children about their own development. I told my students about Davidson's theory and asked how they might refine their social and emotional approaches in the classroom so that everyone would feel happy and healthy. I focused on the idea of being aware because it was closest to asking children to pay particular attention to something, a common request that I often hear parents ask of their child.

When talking with your child about their development—specifically, how they can watch and enhance their social and emotional growth—give relatable examples to support what you are teaching and ask your child to come up with ways to enhance their skills. Be careful not to judge your child's technique. Instead, help them refine their skills through inquiry.

Below are some examples of conversations between my students and me (they called me Ms. Katz) centered on getting them to think about emotional approaches and well-being. These conversations took place over the span of a week and addressed five emotional approaches.

*Ms. Katz:* Our classroom should be a place where we feel safe and happy. Scientists who study the brain believe that we can feel this way when we stop and think about how we act, how we feel, and what we say and do to others. We can ask ourselves questions like, "Is what I'm doing or saying kind?" "How do I feel when I do X?" and "How do I think others feel when I do X?" It is important to *be aware*, to pay attention to, our thoughts and emotions and how they make us act. Some days you will be more aware, or have better attention, than others. Don't get too mad at yourself when you are less aware, just keep trying your best to pay attention and notice your actions.

## 1. Be aware of what people are doing.

*Ms. Katz:* Think about how others might be feeling when you enter their space, before you start talking or playing with them. For example, if Tom notices Chester playing alone with the truck and wants to play too, Tom should pause to think about how Chester is playing and if he wants a friend to join. Why do you think this is important?

*Amalee:* So you don't make them angry. Chester might be busy doing something private. When it's private, they don't want you there. You need to ask first.

*Ms. Katz:* Wondering how our friends want to play and then asking them if you can join is a good plan.

## 2. Be aware of how you act when things don't go your way.

*Ms. Katz:* Notice if you tried to fix the problem and learned from it or if you got upset and decided you were no good. For example, Benny tried three times to cut his paper in half. Once he figured out how to do it, he practiced three more times. He kept trying with patience. Why do you think this is important?

*Calvin:* Because he wanted to know how to do it. You have to practice 'cause sometimes you forget.

*Ms. Katz:* What if you keep trying and can't do it? Sometimes this happens to me, and I become very angry.

*Calvin:* Me too. I get very angry too. I don't want to try it again. I ask for help.

*Ms. Katz:* Calvin, you are very *aware*. It helps to notice what you do so that you can change your actions when you want to.

## 3. Be aware of the messages your body sends you.

*Ms. Katz:* Try to notice when a sensation from your body connects to a feeling or emotion. For example, my friend Joshua had to sing in front of the whole school. When he was on stage, he noticed his chest felt tight because he was nervous. Why is it important to listen to the signals from your body?

*Edie:* Your body talks to you and then you know what to do.

*Ms. Katz:* How do you know what to do?

*Edie:* When I'm scared, my heart beats fast, like this *(making a fist with her left hand and pounding her chest)*. You get real quiet, like this, and then you feel it *(lifting a pointer finger to her lips)*. Shhh!

*Ms. Katz:* Edie, that is a good suggestion to get real quiet and listen to your body before doing something.

**4. Be aware of body language and notice the messages we send without using words.**

*Ms. Katz:* People say a lot without talking by using their face, hands, and body. For example, Russell was scared of the dentist but didn't want her to know. When she asked how he was feeling, Russell said he was okay but didn't look at the dentist. His hands were squeezed into tight fists. Why is it important to notice body language?

*Amir:* Russell didn't like the dentist. He was scared but didn't want to tell her.

*Ms. Katz:* I think the dentist read Russell's body language and cleaned his teeth carefully.

**5. Be aware of your mood and how it is constantly changing.**

*Ms. Katz:* Notice when your mood changes and if it controls your actions. For example, Molly was angry when her mom put jam instead of syrup on her pancake, but then she was happy when her mom put fresh blueberries on top of it. Her mood changed from angry to happy. Why is it important to notice your moods?

*Antony:* She didn't yell at her mom. That would be bad.

*Ms. Katz:* So our moods can cause us to do or say things that might make others sad?

*Antony:* Yes, and then she changed to happy.

After taking a week to explore social and emotional approaches, the class placed posters around the room as a reminder to be aware of, or pay attention to, their emotional approach. The children created symbols alongside the written words to represent each point, which is a useful technique to use if your child does not read yet.

Have conversations with your child that are similar to those above. Help children understand that their emotional approach to experiences and relationships shapes how they think and act. You, too, can place a poster around the house to remind your child of the five emotional approaches. Invite them to draw or write on it, marking it with symbols that help them remember the five points. As you do this, reinforce the following concepts:

- Awareness does not mean there is a right or wrong emotional approach. Instead, emphasize how our thoughts and feelings connect to what we say and do.

- Awareness does not mean judgment. Encourage your child not to judge themselves or others for their emotional approach. Instead, teach them to be curious about why someone might choose that emotional approach.

- Awareness, or paying attention and noticing our actions, shows us our habits. For example, you can help your child notice that recently, when they've played with a certain friend, they become angry and tearful. Ask your child about the response and let them know that it is common to experience a range of emotions when playing with friends and that they can choose their playmates. If they notice that a particular friend makes them feel angry and tearful, maybe it's best to play with someone else for the time being.

These points will help you raise a child who is aware that we all have an emotional approach. Once your child understands that responses to experiences will differ from person to person and that responses are unpredictable, talk with them about nonjudgment.

# 5 EMOTIONAL APPROACHES
## MAKE A POSTER WITH YOUR CHILD

Figure 9

# Teaching Your Child About Nonjudgment

Now that you understand the effects of judgment on how you relate to your child, you can teach your child about nonjudgment. In chapter 2, we talked about language development and effective ways to boost emotional vocabulary. Building on what you learned there, you can intentionally advance your child's verbal and nonverbal language skills to avoid judgment.

To do this, it's helpful to play games, tell stories, or use puppets so children can witness the effects of judgmental language. Using puppets or other storytelling methods provides a context for your child to see the world through the eyes of another instead of asking your child to imagine a conversation, which can be challenging for young children. In chapter 4, for example, we saw that using puppets can illustrate how one's actions can influence others. An alternative to using puppets is to create a story in which your child needs to help resolve a friendship conflict that is filled with judgmental language. It can also be helpful to draw simple pictures to show a scene from the beginning, middle, and end of the story to hold your child's attention. A story could sound something like this:

*Parent:*   Shobi and Duke loved playing together, but one day Shobi became very angry with Duke. They were playing cars, and Duke said that his car was the fastest. Shobi said, "Duke, you're mean! Stop saying my race car is not fast. It is too. Duke, you're a bad guy!" Duke yelled at Shobi, "I'm a good guy!" Now they are no longer friends. Can we help them be friends again?

*(Pause here to ask your child a few questions to help them identify the characters' feelings and actions. Listen carefully to your child's responses because they'll offer a lot of insight into their conflict-resolution skills and how they think about relationships. The goal is to have your child identify judgmental language and think about how it negatively affects relationships.)*

*Parent:*    When Duke said Shobi's car was not fast, Shobi felt sad. Do you agree? When Shobi felt sad, what did he say to Duke?

*(If your child is unsure how to answer, offer a few suggestions. Summarize your child's response, then ask more questions.)*

*Parent:*    Shobi felt sad and mad when Duke said his car was slow, so he said Duke was mean and bad. Did this help? How did Duke react when Shobi told him he was a bad guy?

*(Probe deeper by summarizing your child's response and asking more questions. You want your child to think about how unkind words and actions can shape relationships. Using inquiry helps your child construct their own understanding of the harm caused by judgmental language.)*

*Parent:*    Using unkind language when you're angry with your friend is only going to make your friend angry. What does Shobi want Duke to know? It might help if Shobi told Duke how he was feeling and what he needed by saying, "Duke, when you say my car is not fast, I feel sad. I need my car to be fast too."

*(You can also suggest to your child to pretend to be Shobi and Duke; let them choose the character they'd like to be. By pretending, your child can control the situation and you can intentionally build their emotional language and guide their emotional approach. Listen carefully to what your child says. This will highlight your child's comprehension of the concept that judgmental language negatively impacts relationships.)*

Once you and your child are familiar with how judgmental language affects relationships, you're ready to explore another approach to reducing judgment: questioning the underlying *need* that causes behaviors.

# Assessing Needs to Reduce Judgment

When your child has one of those days when they refuse to get dressed and you are frustrated by everything they do, you can think to yourself, *That's an interesting emotional approach,* then follow with, *I wonder what they need?* As mentioned earlier in the chapter, when you are confused and frustrated by your child's behavior, you may default to judgment. One way to avoid judging your child is to ask yourself what they need and to help your child express their needs.

The way you respond to your child when you are frustrated by their actions influences how they in turn learn to respond to similar situations. When your child strongly disagrees with a friend saying something like, "No! You're wrong, that's not true," encourage them to think about what their friend might need in that situation. Similarly, when they are frustrated by someone's actions, they can ask, "I wonder how my friend feels and what they need?" This is a skill that children can develop over time and with guidance from you and other trusted adults.

As you learned in chapter 4, there are a multitude of influencers, as well as microsystems (family and friends) and macrosystems (society and culture), that shape each individual's emotional approach; however, we all have the same basic needs, such as survival, power, belonging, freedom, and fun.[79] Recognizing that others' actions we do not appreciate may be driven by needs can help reduce judgment. When we respond to our thoughts, feelings, and actions with kindness, curiosity, and nonjudgment, we are creating harmonious relationships. Before talking with your child about their needs, learn to identify theirs and yours. Take Edward, for example, the 5-year-old boy in chapter 3 who didn't want to share with his 3-year-old sister. Edward's parents improved their relationship with their son this way.

Edward's parents were concerned about his self-control with his younger sister. Everything she did seemed to make him angry these days. When she touched his toys, he hollered, "Stop it!" When she entered his room, he screamed, "Get out!" Recently, he told his parents he wanted to move in with Aunt Fiona, who had two dogs and no kids.

When I met with Edward's parents, they recognized that siblings fight, but what concerned them was the shift in Edward's behavior. He used to go out of his way to share with his sister and modeled how to share by negotiating elaborate plans: "You have three minutes with this toy, Elenie, and then it's my turn. I'll play with it for three minutes and then give it back to you. Okay?" Elenie would nod in agreement, willing to do anything her older brother said.

"We can't understand the sudden change in his behavior," his father told me. "He's just so mean to his sister now. He gets frustrated by everything she does."

Edward's mother chimed in with, "Frankly, I'm ready to send him to live with my sister if that's what he wants. I'm tired of his outbursts and his hot temper around the house. He puts all of us on edge."

As I listened to Edward's parents, I could hear how judgments about his emotional approach toward his sister were affecting their feelings toward him and harming their relationship. Gently, we explored their feelings. They were able to acknowledge the judgment and anger in their statements like "He's just so mean now" and "He puts us all on edge," and at first, they were horrified and ashamed by this. But I explained that when parents feel confused by their children's actions, a common response is judgment. When they shifted their viewpoint from judgment to compassion, they recognized that judgment was affecting their relationship with Edward and realized that it was compassion, not judgment, that needed to be extended. They wanted Edward to know that he should treat his sister and others how he wished to be treated.

Next, we talked about Edward's age and his actions relative to his stage of child development. At 5 years old, he'd begun to hide his feelings from his parents and act in ways he believed might upset them, like asking to move in with his aunt. Focusing on development that was common to his age helped his parents shift their viewpoint and ease into a less judgmental state of mind. They understood and accepted that Edward's emotional approach was trying to tell them something, so they started asking themselves, "I wonder what he needs and how can I help?" instead of "Why is Edward so mean to his sister?"

When I asked Edward's parents which need they believed was behind his behavior, they came to the conclusion that he needed some freedom—a chance to be alone without having to always share with his sister. She was younger and had a more tempestuous emotional approach. To keep her calm, they often asked Edward to give in to her demands without thinking about his own needs. Edward's dad, Frank, resisted this idea, believing the approach to be too soft: "Everyone in our family has needs. We can't let Edward go around acting this way because he needs something." I appreciated Frank's candor, but I explained that once they identified Edward's needs, they should identify their own. Frank questioned how to communicate this to a 5-year-old. "This seems complicated," he said. Another excellent point!

So here is a series of three steps to move from judgment to assessment of your child's needs:

1.  Get *mindful* and *roll with patience* (see chapter 6). It is hard to assess needs when you are feeling emotionally or physically charged. These emotions can lead to judgment.

2.  Observe your child's behavior, consider their age and development, and *inquire* about their actions.

3.  *Nonjudgmentally* ask, "What does my child need?" Figure 10 lists some common ways that children express their needs. Keep in mind, however, that certain needs might not be so obvious. Think of yourself as a detective as you try to determine the need behind your child's action.

Once you identify what you think your child needs, your response to their behavior will depend on your parenting style, family culture, and values. Your child wants to feel accepted and safe. They feel this way when you remain warm and responsive to their needs.

# WHAT DOES MY CHILD NEED?
## COMMON WAYS THAT CHILDREN EXPRESS THEIR NEEDS

| Need | Inquire about the Connection to the Need | What to Look for |
|---|---|---|
| PHYSICAL | Are my child's physical needs being met? Are they hungry? Thirsty? Tired? Cold? | Unexpected meltdown in an everyday situation with known people or places, especially around meal/snack times or bedtime/naptime |
| POWER | Is my child feeling competent? Are they feeling effective? Are they trying to communicate their ideas? | Saying 'no;' not listening; doing the opposite action; angrily refusing to do something; expressing a desire to hurt someone or something |
| BELONGING | Is my child feeling connected to others? Are they feeling appreciated? Accepted? Is there sharing and interchange happening? | Wanting to make friends (standing near another child and/or copying what they do); showing emotion when excluded by a group or individual; showing distress when loved ones leave (crying when dropped off at school) |
| FUN | Is my child laughing? Is my child lively? Is my child making discoveries? Is there time for my child to be spontaneous? | Exploring with the five senses: smelling, touching, tasting, seeing, and hearing things; getting wet, dirty, or breaking things |
| FREEDOM | Is my child experiencing independence? Has my child been given choices? Does my child have time to just be? | Intentionally running off; saying 'no' or not listening; excluding others; hoarding or hiding |

Figure 10

After Edward's parents identified his need, they decided that Frank would talk with him. They wanted Edward to know that they recognized he needed some space from his sister, but the way Edward communicated his need was not acceptable. One weekend while they were playing basketball, Frank stopped bouncing the ball and asked Edward to sit down for a moment. First, he recapped some recent incidents and was careful to avoid judgment by restating the observable behavior that he witnessed. "Edward, last week you used a loud voice to tell Elenie to get out of your room. Later you said that you wanted to move in with Aunt Fiona. Do you want to talk about this? What were you feeling and what did you need?"

Edward did not know how to express his needs, which is understandable. What many children do respond to is asking them about their feelings and actions without showing judgment. This shows that you are attuned to their actions and supportive of their needs, and it models how to treat others.

Edward lacked some of the language needed to answer his father's questions, so Frank gave him a prompt. "Were you feeling frustrated, tired, or something else?" With a choice of feelings, Edward responded, "I was mad because I didn't want to share. Elenie breaks my things, and I have to wait until my birthday to get new ones." Frank listened carefully. Not only did Edward need some independence, as his parents suspected, but he was feeling powerless, too. "Did you want to go to Aunt Fiona's house so that you could play with your things without worrying that they'd break?" Frank asked. Edward nodded.

"Thank you for telling me your feelings and what you need, Edward. Maybe we should find a few toys to share with Elenie that you don't mind if she breaks." Edward nodded again. Frank continued, "And now, what about the yelling and the door slamming? In our home, we don't slam doors; it's not safe and it could break the door. The next time you're mad, what will you do?"

"I will close the door nicely, Dad."

Frank smiled. "Thanks. Now let's play ball."

After this conversation, Frank shared with me that it was the first time in a long time that he'd felt at ease talking with his son. "It felt different not to judge him. I wasn't angry at all. I felt really calm." Frank noticed that judgment escalated his negative feelings toward his son and that being nonjudgmental made him feel more connected to Edward. This isn't always easy to do, but it's a game changer. In fact, one of the most challenging tasks as a parent is figuring out what your child needs to feel safe and happy, as this can shift from day to day, sometimes from minute to minute.

In this chapter, we explored how to focus on your child's needs as a way to avoid judgment—shame, blame, and criticism. An important part of this process is talking with your child about their emotional approach and how to pay attention to it. Now that you know how to nonjudgmentally observe and interact with your child, let's explore the last step in the MIND framework—D for deciding how you will respond to conflict.

# CHAPTER 8

# Decide How You Will Respond to Your Child's Actions

Tyra was chatting up a storm in her stroller, asking "Dat? Dis? Doh? Doh?!" as she and her mom, Claudia, walked home from the park. Claudia loved that her 15-month-old daughter was curious, but at times, she felt exhausted and overwhelmed. Responding to Tyra's curiosities sometimes left her feeling she had no time to focus on her own.

Claudia stopped at the supermarket to pick up a few items for dinner. The market detour was intended to be quick and easy, but it didn't happen the way Claudia imagined. Once they entered the store, Tyra asked for the name of everything she saw. After all, being curious is the job of a 15-month-old. She pointed to bags of rice and frozen peas, asking, "Dis?" Claudia wearily answered, "Peas, Tyra, peas."

The cereal aisle especially piqued Tyra's curiosity, and she wanted to know the name of each item. A particularly colorful box caught Tyra's eye, so she reached out from her stroller and grabbed it. Holding the big box thrilled her, and she began to shake it. It made a rattling sound. Again and again. She giggled and cried out, "Dis, dis!" But Claudia didn't laugh back. She snatched the box from Tyra and placed it back on the shelf. There was a moment of silence before the storm. Suddenly, Tyra wailed, "Moh, moh!" Claudia responded, "You can't shake the box like that. The cereal box is not an instrument."

Tyra continued to wail. Her cries became louder and louder as she kicked her legs and flailed her arms from her stroller. "Moh, moh!" She pointed to the box and said, "Dis, dis!" Her cries grabbed the attention of other shoppers. Claudia blushed and felt ashamed by her daughter's sudden outburst. Not wanting to attract more attention, she walked briskly to the checkout line, justifying her actions to herself: *Tyra needs to know this is not okay. She can't shake and break things at the market; she needs limits.*

As Claudia reached the checkout line, she thought about the MIND framework, which she'd recently learned about in a parenting workshop. She tried to be *mindful.* She paused and took a breath, then mentally *inquired* what she could do at this moment. She felt ashamed for snapping at Tyra and embarrassed by her behavior, noticing that she was *not judging* Tyra, but was judging herself. She needed to keep rolling with patience until she felt better—she needed time to *decide* how to respond to her actions as well as to Tyra's.

When you feel frustrated by your child's actions, it is difficult to decide how to respond. You want to do so in a manner that is *timely* and *clear.* Deciding includes both thinking about your response *and* acting intentionally. When your reaction is timely, it shows that you have thought about the best time to respond to your child's recent behavior to change their future actions. Once you have determined when to respond, you need to be clear by choosing words that your child understands and relates to in order to bring about change. Making a decision requires pausing before you react to what your child says and does and taking into consideration their emotional approach and developmental stage so that they fully comprehend what is expected of them and why. The stories in this chapter will show the MIND framework in action, paying particular attention to the decision-making step.

# Timeliness: When Is the Best Time to Respond to Your Child?

Being timely requires being mindful and observant so that you know when to react to what your child says and does. It involves asking, "Is this the right time to respond? Or should I wait until later?" You have a greater chance of impacting your child's emotional development when your child is at ease and attentive. To evaluate the best time to respond, it helps to think about timeliness in three ways: before, during, and after an incident.

## Before an Incident: Troubleshooting Ahead of Time to Avoid a Meltdown

This type of thinking is best done before transitioning from one experience to another, with the goal of informing your child that a transition is coming. For example, reminding your child that they will have to stop playing with their train set soon because bath time is coming helps them prepare to stop what they are doing. When a child is engrossed in an activity, they typically are not thinking about what is coming next. Letting children know ahead of time what to expect prepares them for the next activity. These questions can be helpful to ask as you manage transitions with your child:

- *How much time does my child need to transition?*

  You know your child best. Some children transition easily, while others find it more challenging. Giving advance warning in the form of a countdown can help your child with transitions. For instance, tell them five minutes ahead of time, then give a two-minute warning, then a thirty-second warning. Talk to your child in the same way you appreciate being spoken to—think about your tone of voice, words, and body language.

- *How will I help my child transition smoothly?*

  If your child needs a little boost to make a transition, kindly work alongside them by asking, "How would you like me to help? Which train should I put away first?" This line of questioning offers some power to your child because they get a chance to tell you what to do. It's important to remember that children need to feel in control and heard.

- *Have I decided on the consequences if my child resists?*

  Clearly and kindly tell your child what to expect if they continue to resist making the transition, then follow through with the consequence. "It's time for your bath now. I'd like to help you put the trains away, but if I tidy up alone, the trains will be placed on the desk and they will stay there for a while." In this case, the consequence is purposely more open-ended. The trains staying on the desk "for a while" is different from taking the trains away for a month. It's open-ended because the goal is to get your child to take a bath. Making threats about the trains will distract you from the goal and escalate the situation. However, saying the trains will stay on the desk for a while gives you time to determine when the trains will move from your desk back to the play space and how to reinforce what happens when it's time to clean up their toys.

Another way to support your child's emotion regulation is finding opportunities to talk with them when they are calm about situations they will likely encounter. For example, imagine you are at the park pushing your child on the swing. Next to you is another child, roughly the same age, hollering and crying because their mom can't come over to push them on the swing. Discreetly ask your child about what they observed:

- What do you think made the child upset?

- What could you tell the child to do instead of screaming?

These conversations can help prepare your child to face similar situations by providing ideas for how to respond.

## During an Incident: Shifting Your Child's Attention in the Moment

You certainly do your best to troubleshoot ahead of time to avoid meltdowns, but as you know, they still happen. Knowing how to handle an emotional outburst in the moment takes patience and understanding. The following story illustrates one approach to responding to a meltdown in an everyday scenario, during a family dinner.

Kate finished setting the table. Her mother, sister, brother-in-law, and their children were coming for dinner. Kate found it stressful to have her family at the house, but it was her mother's birthday and she wanted to cook a special dinner to celebrate. Kate glanced at the clock. She still had thirty minutes before everyone arrived, including her husband, Malcolm, and their son 6-year-old son, Cole, who were at soccer practice. The food was ready and the table was set, but was the playroom tidy?

Kate walked into the playroom and saw the fort made from blankets, chairs, pillows, and an empty box. Cole had spent hours earlier in the week putting it together as a space for him to play and read. Kate dismantled the fort and threw out the box. Now the room looked presentable.

The doorbell rang. Kate opened the door to greet her family. After a quick round of hugs, the kids dashed off to the playroom while the adults had a glass of wine and cheese. A few minutes later, Cole and Malcolm walked in through the garage door. Upon Kate's request, Cole hugged his grandmother and then ran off to join his cousins. Moments later, he started yelling, "Who wrecked my fort? Where are my things?" He ran out of the playroom looking for his mother, waving his arms and stomping his feet.

Staring at his mother, eyes squinted, he hollered, "Did you wreck my fort, Mom? What's wrong with you?"

The room went silent. Kate was mortified. How could she respond to Cole's outburst in front of guests? Kate did not respond immediately. She was too angry to talk, and this sort of anger caused her to act in ways she knew she would regret. But she couldn't have Cole standing in the living room flailing his arms and hollering, either. She took a deep breath in, relaxed her shoulders, and wiggled her fingers (being mindful). The anger had made her feel jittery, and she thought it was best to stay quiet, which was a good choice. Kate got close to Cole and calmly said, "Let's go to your room for a moment." Cole nodded his head in compliance as a few tears streamed down his face.

As they entered the room, Kate said, "Let's both take a time-in." Cole agreed. Kate sat on his bed and took a few minutes to gather her thoughts. Cole picked up an illustrated book on how things work and sat on the floor. Now was not the time to talk about respectful language. She would do this later, maybe even in a few days, after she and Malcolm had a chance to share their views on what they wanted Cole to know about respect (practicing both timeliness and decision making). Next, she thought about Cole's current needs. After his outburst, he was likely embarrassed and needed to feel a sense of belonging and acceptance from his family. So Kate apologized for taking the fort down without telling him and explained that she wanted to clean the house before company arrived. Cole listened. Then she explicitly told him they would discuss what had happened and her need to feel respected. Kate was preparing Cole for a future conversation about a consequence for his outburst, which would happen at a later time. "Would you like to keep reading or join your cousins now?" she asked in conclusion.

Cole said he would come out soon. As Kate left his room, she took a deep breath before facing her family. She chose to say nothing about what had happened. Kate felt good about her response and knowing she would take time to talk with her son later.

Responding to your child during an incident often involves knowing how to shift your child's attention in the moment. In the case of Kate and Cole, they both needed to take some time away from others—they took a "time-in"—to control strong emotions. A time-in offers an opportunity for your child to check in with their feelings and desires and how they express them. It also provides time for you to assure your child that you care about them and that you are available to listen when you are both calm. Many parents give themselves time-ins too. They ask for time to be quiet to process their emotions.

A time-in is not a punishment; rather, it's a chance to practice self-awareness and self-regulation. It's a space in which to notice what it feels like to go from feeling tense and angry to feeling calm. How does a time-in differ from a time-out? A time-out is when children are separated from others because of bad behavior, as described to me by a 7-year-old: "A time-out is when you misbehave and then you have to be alone. I don't want to tell you why I have had time-outs. I don't want to say. Time-out is bad. You're bad when you have them." A time-in, on the other hand, is a span for understanding.

Guide your child to understand that you still love and care for them. Explain to your child that they are not bad, but that their choice of actions could have been different and that they need to pause in a neutral space—a safe place that alleviates their anger and frustration, such as their bedroom—and take a time-in to:

- Consider how their actions affect others

- Try to name the emotion(s) they are experiencing

- Identify any tension (a feeling of tightness) in their body and see if they can release it

- Listen to their thoughts (that is, what they're saying to themselves about the experience)

When you ask your child to take a time-in, be consistent with how you respond to their actions. Before telling your child to take a time-in:

- Determine the place you will ask them to stay, such as their room or another spot in your home.

- Ask if your child is okay on their own or if it would help to stay with them. Some children like to take time by themselves, while others find it scary and isolating. The goal is not to scare your child, but to get your child to regulate their emotions and to consider how their actions may harm others.

- Suggest things your child can do during a time-in. For example, if your child is very upset or frustrated, they might be yelling, crying, or breaking things. Your child needs to understand the limits of what they can and cannot do—breaking toys or tearing books is not okay, but appropriately venting their feelings is okay. Here are a few acceptable options:

  - Pounding a pillow, screaming into a blanket, or yelling at a stuffed animal

  - Crumpling paper, mashing Play-Doh or clay, or squeezing something soft

  - Exercising, stretching, or jumping up and down

  - Counting breath cycles, singing, or listening to music

  - Sitting quietly with a book, drawing, or playing with a toy

The time-in is over when your child is in a neutral and calm state. If your child is on their own, check in with them from time to time. If you are sitting alongside your child, try to remain quiet until they have balanced their emotions. This gives your child time to settle down on their own and to experience how emotions shift and change as time passes. Give your child time to discover their own self-soothing techniques and to build skills to regulate their emotions. When the time is right, help them process what they experienced. Offer relatable examples to support their learning and ask your child about the techniques they chose to calm down. Be careful not to judge your child's techniques. Instead, help them refine their skills through asking them questions. For example, "How many books did you look at until you started to feel calm?"

## After an Incident: Reflecting on Your Reaction

Taking time to reflect on your reaction to your child's behavior can help you respond more mindfully in the future. Think back to Tyra's meltdown at the supermarket and how this differed from Kate and Cole's experience. Both parents successfully implemented MIND framework steps, Claudia just needed a little more "post-incident time" to fully process what happened and fully benefit from the framework.

Recall that Claudia, like Kate, scanned her body for tension and inquired about what she was telling herself, trying as best she could not to judge herself too harshly. What she noticed was a sense of shame— she was concerned that the people in the supermarket would judge her parenting, but she was also ashamed of herself for losing her patience with her daughter. Throughout Tyra's outburst, Claudia tried to roll with patience, but her feelings were getting the best of her. Nevertheless, once Claudia became aware of her shame, the acknowledgment gave her more control over her reaction, and in the end, she decided to pause for a while before responding to Tyra.

Several hours later—when mother and daughter were both back at home and calm—Claudia was ready to reflect on the incident. What was the best approach to take with Tyra about their last visit to the market so that their next visit would be more pleasant for both of them? At 15 months, Tyra was just starting to talk and her memory for past events was still developing (see chapter 3), so trying to have a reasoned conversation with her toddler about what had happened was likely not the best tactic.

Instead, Claudia thought about the timing of the trip to the market and realized they were on their way home for lunch. Tyra was hungry! Of course! By incorporating inquiry into her daughter's needs and then nonjudgmentally observing the circumstances of the incident, Claudia was able to answer the question "I wonder what Tyra needed?" So the next time they were due for a trip to the supermarket, Claudia would pack a snack for Tyra to munch on and (hopefully) keep her hands and eyes busy.

## Clarity: What Is the Clearest Way to Respond to Your Child?

Being timely with your responses helps you and your child better regulate your emotions. In addition to being timely, though, being clear is essential as you work to decide how best to respond to your child's actions and behaviors—being clear about boundary setting *and* being clear about your messaging.

### Setting Clear Boundaries for Your Child

Putting in place clear and consistent limits for your child helps them anticipate how an experience might unfold. Boundaries let children know what you expect from them and, in turn, teach them to choose actions and behaviors that will more likely lead to desired outcomes.

When boundaries are not clear, your child does not know what they should be doing, and that makes it hard for them to transition from one experience to the next. When you say no to your child, try to tell them what you expect from them and what will happen if they cross the line. For example, instead of saying, "Don't throw your food," you can ask your child to keep their food on their plate and let them know that if they throw it, they will be asked to leave the table.

Children themselves understand that rules and boundaries are helpful. Knowing what they should and should not do allows children to explore and gather information about the world and to assess when they have gone too far. It is up to you to determine how far you will allow your child to explore and to inform them of the limits you have set.

Here's a conversation I had with a few of my 6-year-old students that highlights why they value boundaries.

*Ms. Katz:* Why do parents and teachers make rules for children?

*James:* We don't know what to do, so our parents and teachers help us.

*Ms. Katz:* Why don't you know what to do?

*Tamara:* We're still little.

*Mitch:* We aren't old enough yet.

*Ms. Katz:* How long should rules stay the same?

*Kyra:* They have to stay the same a long time so we can follow them. They change when it's our birthday. We know more when we get older.

*Mitch:* Our parents trust us, so we can do more.

*Ms. Katz:* How do the rules change when your parents and teachers trust you?

*Tamara:* You can go downstairs by yourself in the morning.

*Ms. Katz:* When you go downstairs, what do you do? Do you eat ice cream for breakfast?

*Children:* (*Laughing*) No!

*James:* You don't eat the ice cream because then your parents won't trust you and then you have more rules.

*Mitch:* (*Summarizing the conversation*) When you're small, you practice with more rules and then you have your birthday and you get less rules because you're older and you can do more and you know what to do and people trust you.

This exchange shows that children recognize why adults set boundaries and that rules can change as they develop and can take on more responsibility. Having conversations with your child about the rules and boundaries in your family offers them independence (which most children yearn for) within limits. It shows your child that you trust them and believe they have the self-awareness and self-regulation tools to stay within the boundaries you set.

## Sending Clear and Meaningful Messages to Your Child

Word choice matters when you talk to your child. This might seem obvious, but parents may not always pay attention to what they say and how they say it. Because children are learning how to communicate and evaluate how their actions will make others feel, it's important to make sure they understand what you say. For example, when parents tell their child to "be kind," they may not be aware that their child doesn't understand the concept or what kindness looks like in action. Children, like adults, understand concepts better when they have a personal connection with them—when they are meaningful. To help your child understand positive social skills, such as kindness, ask yourself the following questions:

- *Have I chosen words and phrases that are familiar to my child? Am I building on my child's prior knowledge?*

Instead of "What's wrong with you? Can't you see your sister is waiting? Your behavior is unacceptable," try something specific and simple like, "It's time for your little sister to take a turn now." A young child may not easily grasp the concept of unacceptable behavior, but they know exactly what you mean when you remind them someone else needs a turn.

- *Am I teaching this concept in a fun and meaningful way?*

  Giving your child a long list of things they cannot do because they are disrespectful may not be very impactful in helping them understand how to respect another person. Try drawing or writing a story instead that features your child's favorite characters being disrespected. Ask your child about what's wrong in the story, how each character is feeling, and how they would resolve the situation.

- *Did my child hear the message accurately?*

  Ask your child to retell or reenact what they heard, then correct any misconceptions they may have. Instead of fruitlessly asking, "Did you hear me?" many times over, say: "How many minutes do you have left to play before cleanup time? Which three things do you need to clean up?"

The next time you find yourself frustrated and perplexed by your child's response to what you've asked them to do, ask yourself whether your child understood the words you used, how they interpreted them, and whether you simplified the concept in a fun and meaningful way.

# Putting Theory into Practice When Deciding How to Respond

Now that you're equipped to be both timely and clear with your child in the decision-making phase of the MIND framework, let's take a look at two versions of the same story—one that applies the framework and one that does not, leading to significantly different outcomes.

## The Unplayful Playdate: Take One

Jay was in the kitchen cutting some carrot sticks and apple slices for snacks when he heard his 4-year-old son, Martin, yelling at his friends in the backyard. "I'm the king of the swing, and I say you can only swing when I give you the command."

Andrew (4 years old) pushed back. "Why? How come you're the king?"

Martin stared at Andrew with his hands resting on his hips.

Rosie (also 4 years old), confused by the game, asked, "Who am I, then?"

Martin's tone grew louder. "I said I'm the king and the king makes the rules, so you have to follow what I say. If you keep asking, there will be no swinging today. The swing will be closed!" Martin lifted his hands off his hips for a moment and tightened his fists. Andrew and Rosie looked at each other and quietly walked away from Martin.

Jay watched Martin and his friends from the kitchen window. He was angry and dismayed. *What's wrong with Martin? Why is he so bossy?*

Jay stopped what he was doing and went outside. "Martin, come here for a moment!" he demanded. With a look of disappointment on his face, Jay told his son, "I'll send your friends home if you are not kind to them. Now go play and be nice." Martin stomped his foot on the ground and walked away.

Observing your child behave in a way that you disapprove of can make you question whether your child knows how to treat others and make you doubt your parenting skills. Jay believed that all Martin had to do to be kind was to do as he was told. But did Martin even understand *how* to be kind?

# The Unplayful Playdate: Take Two

Let's reimagine this playdate scenario. In this version, Jay uses the MIND framework to respond to Martin's behavior.

Jay watched Martin and his friends playing outside from the kitchen window. He was dismayed at how his son was behaving. *What's wrong with Martin? Why is he so bossy?* Jay's shame made him angry, but he paused before acting on that anger. He heard his judging mind in action and noticed he was clenching his teeth. Mindfully, he let his jaw relax as he weighed whether he should intervene or not. He decided to stay out of the playdate in the hopes that Martin would learn from the experience.

Jay returned to slicing carrots and apples while he focused on his breathing. Every now and then, he'd scan his jaw for tension. Watching the children through the window, he monitored the situation. Martin was still on the swing, but after some time, he went over to his friends, who were pretending to be puppies. Instead of asking to join their game, he took on a role in their pretend play. Rosie threw Martin a stick and he fetched it, acting like a puppy.

When Jay came out with the snacks, he didn't mention the incident he'd witnessed. "Here's some food for the hungry dogs!" He let the kids carry on. Even though Martin had become kinder to his friends on his own, Jay still felt it was important to talk with him about how to be a kind host.

Jay had noticed a pattern with Martin. When he tried to talk about an incident right after it happened (timeliness), Martin wouldn't listen. Recently, they'd been having their best conversations during bath time, so he chose (decided) to broach the subject during bath time that evening. To make the concept fun and meaningful (clarity), Jay planned to use the toys in the tub to reenact what happened in the backyard and ask Martin to offer suggestions on how to be kind and make friends feel welcome. Asking Martin to add his opinions (inquiry) would give Jay insight into how well Martin understood his point.

In the bathtub that night, Martin was preoccupied by dunking his washcloth in the water and pretending it was a rain cloud. Jay quickly felt frustrated and worried that things wouldn't go as planned, but he (mindfully) rolled with patience instead of interrupting Martin's playtime. When Martin was finished with the washcloth, Jay took the opportunity to use some of Martin's favorite bath toys to act out what had happened in the backyard.

Shark:     (To his friend the starfish) Bath time is fun! Look at all of these bubbles! I'm the king of bubbles, and only the king can use this cup.

Starfish:  Oh, that looks fun. I want to play with that cup too.

Shark:     You can only play with the cup when I say so.

Jay asked Martin how the starfish might be feeling and if he could tell the shark how to be a kinder friend. Martin responded that the shark needed to give the starfish a choice instead of telling him what to do. Jay then invited Martin to make up his own story with the shark and the starfish. In Martin's rendition, the shark asked the starfish if he wanted to play with the spoon or the measuring cup and gave him what he wanted.

The second version of Jay and Martin's story illustrates that parents can have well-timed and playful conversations with their children to communicate a concept meaningfully. Guiding your child during everyday activities they enjoy can help your child learn to express their thoughts and needs and provides an opportunity for you to model language that promotes strong social-emotional skills. The D component of the MIND framework in particular reminds you to consciously decide to build your child's social-emotional development by responding to their actions in a timely and clear way. In sum:

- When you are timely and clear, you can anticipate how your child might respond to an experience and troubleshoot how to shift your child's attention when they are upset and frustrated.

- When you set boundaries for your child, they are able to reflect upon whether their actions fall within or outside of those bounds.

- By having meaningful conversations with your child about their behavior, you can positively influence their social-emotional development.

The stories in this chapter showed parents with toddlers, preschoolers, and school-age children practicing the MIND framework. Each example serves as a reminder for you to blend the MIND framework with the research in part one on children's development of theory of mind, language, executive function skills, and how family culture influences your child.

Combining knowledge of child development with the techniques of the MIND framework—mindfulness, inquiry, nonjudgment, and decision making—offers a parenting approach that nurtures your child's social-emotional development. Use the MIND framework to parent in a manner that makes your child feel safe, accepted, and cared for and that builds a harmonious relationship with your child.

# Conclusion

In the popular movie *Inside Out,* viewers get a peek inside the mind of protagonist Riley as she navigates the difficult experience of moving to a new city with her family. Emotions such as joy, sadness, and anger are personified as characters who grapple to take control of Riley's thoughts and shape how she perceives the world and how she expresses herself. Similarly, our message throughout this book has been that you can support your child's social and emotional development by helping them understand how their thoughts and feelings work inside their head and how those shape their interactions with other people.

Raising a socially and emotionally intelligent child involves seeing your child's actions through the lens of their development and pausing to respond to their needs intentionally versus impulsively. Each child develops in their own way, in their own time, and perceives experiences through their own lens. The same holds true for you as a person and a parent. We are always learning, developing, and growing—this is central to our humanity.

There is no perfect parent, and there is no perfect child. There is, however, the miracle of human development and how the mind perceives experiences. Beginning at birth, we read the emotional cues of others to determine how to connect with one another. Social-emotional intelligence lies at the foundation of child development, and what you do and say plays a critical role in how your child views the world and reacts to experiences.

We developed the MIND framework to help parents see the world as their children perceive it at different stages of their development and for parents to develop a deeper awareness of their parenting so they can help their children understand their reactions to their social and emotional experiences. Our hope is that the framework gives you a set of tools to help you appreciate and celebrate your child's development and imbues you with confidence to enhance your child's social-emotional development.

In our experience working with families both in and out of educational settings, we've found time and again that teaching parents how to view situations from their child's perspective changes their approach to parenting. Remember Rene and her 4-year-old daughter, Angela, from the very start of the book? Rene worried that her daughter didn't have any friends and shared, "I just want Angela to be happy. Often, she comes home and tells me she feels sad at preschool because other girls won't play with her. When I tell her to find someone else to play with, she snaps at me and says that I'm dumb." Rene wanted to fix the "friend problem" and became frustrated by what she perceived as Angela's inability to make friends.

Once Rene understood the progression of ToM in relation to other key aspects of child development and applied the MIND framework, she approached Angela's sadness differently. Rene used mindfulness techniques to recognize and become comfortable with the feeling of wanting to fix Angela's sadness. The more balanced Rene felt, the more accepting she was of her feelings and Angela's. Instead of telling Angela what to do and how to feel, she learned to ask herself helpful questions:

- How are Angela's thoughts, feelings, and actions impacting her relationships with others?

- What is Angela assuming about the point of view (beliefs or desires) of others?

- How can I help shape Angela's experience so that she remains kind and open-minded toward herself and others?

- Which of my actions are helpful to Angela and what do I want to model?

These questions helped Rene focus on the present moment and avoid shame and blame. There were times when Rene could not focus or decide what she wanted to model and how. During those times, she reminded herself to roll with patience, knowing that she needed to wait until she was in the right frame of mind before responding.

When Rene talked with Angela about her feelings, she made the conversations meaningful by telling playful stories featuring characters who had similar friendship struggles. Together, they came up with strategies for the characters to make friends at school. There were times, however, when Rene couldn't get through to Angela at all. When that happened, Rene proactively reached out to Angela's teachers for advice about what to do.

Over time, Rene noticed her relationship with Angela changing. Rene began to laugh more and, in general, her mood felt lighter. Instead of spending time making assumptions about how Angela felt, she took the time to observe Angela and ask her about her experiences. At times, when Rene felt overwhelmed or angry, she explicitly told Angela that she needed to pause, observe her own emotions, and practice patience before helping her daughter.

The MIND framework helps you parent more patiently and proactively while simultaneously fostering your child's emotional balance and social awareness. To measure and monitor your child's social-emotional development, consider: (1) how and when your child begins to think about mental states, such as thoughts, feelings, beliefs, and desires; (2) how to explicitly talk to your child about their behavior while they are young and the seeds of social-emotional awareness are being sown; and (3) how to be mindful and intentional about your responses to your child's actions.

During your child's early years, they are developing a theory about what the mind is. Gradually, they learn that they have thoughts, beliefs, desires, and intentions that drive their actions and that these mental states differ from those of others. In the early grade school years, your child learns that individuals can have different ideas about the same situation and that there is a stream of consciousness, with the mind constantly full of thoughts and ideas.

The ability to comprehend mental states is complex. Each time you ask your child to control their behaviors and emotions, you're asking them to combine many skills that they are learning in tandem. They are learning to communicate effectively, control their impulses, and think about another person's point of view. That's no easy task! So before you react to your child's actions, try to pause and ask whether they have the developmental ability to do what you think they are capable of doing.

It's important to remember that children learn through doing. To promote positive social skills and broaden your child's emotional awareness, look for opportunities for your child to consider the point of view of others, including peers, siblings, teachers, and anyone else who influences them. Talk with your child about their inner world and help them understand that thoughts, beliefs, and intentions guide our actions (which includes what we say) and that the way we react to others has the power to comfort or to cause harm. Use our suggested teaching strategies such as puppets, role-play, drawing, and stories to make conversations with your child engaging and memorable.

There will be days when the skills in the MIND framework will be easy to access. Other days will be more challenging. For example, there may be times when puppet shows and the feelings jar appeal to your child, and then suddenly they become tired of them. This is normal. When fear, restlessness, and doubt get the best of you, remember that your child's social and emotional learning follows a continuum of development with lots of ups and downs along the way.

Although each letter of the MIND framework corresponds to a set of skills and actions, applying the framework to your parenting is a nonlinear and interconnected process. I (Rachael) noticed that it was hard to slow down and pause. It took me a long time to learn to be mindful, whereas inquiry came more naturally. My thinking slowed down when I asked questions and was able to turn off my inner, critical voice that always had something negative to say about my parenting or my child. Inquiry helps with nonjudgment, so I often blended these two skills. When I felt calm, I took five deep breaths, and to remain in the moment and stay mindful, I counted each one.

When my children were young, I often found myself using the mantra we've repeatedly offered here—"Roll with patience"—especially when my children had a meltdown while I was trying to do something else, like getting dinner ready or responding to email. I would get so frustrated that I'd want to scream or hurl something. It seemed the more frantic I was, the more meltdowns my kids would have. When this happened, I felt my body tighten, so I learned to pause and gather some information about what I was feeling and what was happening around me. Often, my body would tense up even more, and I'd just repeat, "Roll with it, patience, wait, watch, observe, keep rolling ..." This self-talk served as a lifeline that I relied on even through the teenage years.

We realize that applying the skills in the MIND framework to your daily life can feel intimidating, particularly when the times you need them the most are the times when your child is testing their limits. Be patient with yourself and know that making mistakes is part of the process of transforming your approach to parenting and raising an emotionally intelligent child. Remember to celebrate the "small stuff," like quiet moments reflecting with your child, talking about how a character might be feeling when reading a book or watching a movie, and witnessing your child comfort a friend who is feeling sad.

Think of what the world would be like if we all took the time to talk with our children about their inner world, helped them understand how the mind develops, and taught them to respect other people's minds. Imagine how socially and emotionally intelligent humans would be if, during our early years, parents guided and modeled how to be intentional and compassionate with their reactions, respecting everyone's emotional approach to their experiences. Wouldn't we all be a lot kinder to one another and ourselves? Children are our future. If we want to live in a world of compassionate and thoughtful people, then it's up to us to do our best to raise socially and emotionally intelligent children.

# Acknowledgments

As first-time book authors, we often brought to mind the proverb "It takes a village" as we worked on this book. As researchers and educators, we have written countless papers and articles, parent letters, and lesson plans, but we learned (very quickly) that writing a book is a completely different process. As such, we are grateful for the invaluable help and guidance that many colleagues and friends provided along the way.

We want to thank the many children we have taught and gathered research from over the years. By sharing their questions, ideas, joys, and fears, each of these children taught us how to see the world through their eyes. A special word of thanks goes to the parents who felt safe enough to share their struggles with us and were willing to use the MIND framework as an alternative parenting approach. We loved your feedback and honesty on the techniques that came easy, those you struggled with, and those that you thought were asking for too much time or effort. You made our book better.

We have been fortunate to work with and learn from child development researchers who have inspired us with their innovative ways of getting inside a child's head. Without your studies, we could not help parents understand how the mind develops and how young children view the world. Additionally, we acknowledge the ancient meditation practices that provide the foundation for the MIND framework and greatly influenced Rachael's teaching practices.

Our editors Ryan Buresh and Jennifer Holder at New Harbinger Publications guided us on how to translate our professional knowledge and research experience into an accessible and practical framework for parenting. We are especially grateful for their patience and good humor throughout the book-writing process and never making us feel like we were asking too many questions. Many thanks to Amy Eisenmann and Katie Kennedy, who read and commented on each chapter, lending valuable advice from both professional and personal perspectives. And an enthusiastic high five to Karen Caparo, our graphic artist, who brought our ideas and research to life throughout the book with her creative eye.

Although it may seem odd to thank a place, the Bay Area Discovery Museum and, in particular, our talented former colleagues there, greatly influenced our thinking and ideas captured in this book. The stunning views of the Golden Gate Bridge provided the perfect backdrop to observe children engaging in exploratory play and to discover what inspires and challenges them.

Rachael is grateful to her family, Micah, Nina, and Jacob. During Jacob's and Nina's early years, they gently reminded her they were her children and not her students. This prompted her to tweak classroom teaching techniques so they could be used at home. While writing this book, her family cheered her on with "You got this, Mom!" which carried her through the challenging moments. Micah continues to remind her of the importance of being an early childhood teacher. Her parents, Solomon and Judith, and her brother, Noah, showed her the joys of creativity and the benefits of having a steady, focused mind.

Helen would like to thank her loud, crazy, and loving family. She is forever grateful to Dave, Grace, and Ruby, who make life more like a roller coaster than a merry-go-round (inspired by the movie *Parenthood*). Her parents, Hla and Sara, and her brothers, Walter and Mike, set the foundation for putting family first and talking about the next meal before finishing what's on their plate (they are a traditional Chinese family in that sense). She's also been lucky to have friends and "sisters" from many phases of her life who have supported her through the toughest of times and been there to celebrate life's sweetest moments. There are too many to list, but you know who you are.

# Notes

1   Wellman, H. M. 2011. "Developing a Theory of Mind." In
    *The Blackwell Handbook of Cognitive Development*, edited by
    U. Goswami, 258–284. 2nd ed. Hoboken, NJ: Wiley-Blackwell.

2   Doherty, M. 2008. *Theory of Mind: How Children Understand
    Others' Thoughts and Feelings*. New York: Psychology Press.

3   Flavell, J. H. 2004. "Theory-of-Mind Development: Retrospect
    and Prospect." *Merrill-Palmer Quarterly* 50: 274–290.

4   Slaughter, V. 2015. "Theory of Mind in Infants and Young
    Children: A Review." *Australian Psychologist* 50: 169–172.

5   Wellman, H. M. 2011. "Developing a Theory of Mind."
    In *The Blackwell Handbook of Cognitive Development*, edited by
    U. Goswami, 258–284. 2nd ed. Hoboken, NJ: Wiley-Blackwell.

6   Wellman, H. M., D. Cross, and J. Watson. 2001. "Meta-Analysis
    of Theory-of-Mind Development: The Truth About False Belief."
    *Child Development* 72: 655–684.

7   Baron-Cohen, S., A. M. Leslie, and U. Frith. 1985. "Does the
    Autistic Child Have a 'Theory of Mind'?" *Cognition* 21: 37–46.

8   Adamson, L. B., and J. E. Frick. 2003. "The Still Face: A History
    of a Shared Experimental Paradigm." *Infancy* 4: 451–473.

9   Woodward, A. L., J. A. Sommerville, and J. J. Guajardo. 2001.
    "How Infants Make Sense of Intentional Action." In *Intentions
    and Intentionality: Foundations of Social Cognition*, edited by
    B. F. Malle, L. J. Moses, and D. A. Baldwin, 69–85. Cambridge,
    MA: MIT Press.

10  Meltzoff, A. N. 1995. "Understanding the Intentions of Others:
    Re-enactment of Intended Acts by 18-Month-Old Children."
    *Developmental Psychology* 31: 838–850.

11  Repacholi, B. M., and A. Gopnik. 1997. "Early Reasoning About Desires: Evidence from 14- and 18-Month-Olds." *Developmental Psychology* 33: 12–21.

12  Wellman, H. M., and J. D. Woolley. 1990. "From Simple Desires to Ordinary Beliefs: The Early Development of Everyday Psychology." *Cognition* 35: 245–275.

13  Ibid.

14  Peskin, J. 1992. "Ruse and Representations: On Children's Ability to Conceal Information." *Developmental Psychology* 28: 84–89.

15  Chandler, M. J., and D. Helm. 1984. "Developmental Changes in the Contribution of Shared Experience to Social Role-Taking Competence." *International Journal of Behavioral Development* 7: 145–156.

16  Lagattuta, K. H., H. J. Kramer, K. Kennedy, K. Hjortsvang, D. Goldfarb, and S. Tashjian. 2015. "Beyond Sally's Missing Marble: Further Development in Children's Understanding of Mind and Emotion in Middle Childhood." In *Advances in Child Development and Behavior*, edited by J. B. Benson, 185–217. Philadelphia: Elsevier.

17  Flavell, J. H., F. L. Green, and E. R. Flavell. 1993. "Children's Understanding of the Stream of Consciousness." *Child Development* 64: 387–398.

18  Kuhl, P. K. 2004. "Early Language Acquisition: Cracking the Speech Code." *Nature Reviews Neuroscience* 5: 831–843.

19  Kuhl, P. K., E. Stevens, A. Hayashi, T. Deguchi, S. Kiritani, and P. Iverson. 2006. "Infants Show a Facilitation Effect for Native Language Phonetic Perception Between 6 and 12 Months." *Developmental Science* 9: F13–F21.

20  Ibid.

21  Bergelson, E., and D. Swingley. 2012. "At 6–9 Months, Human Infants Know the Meanings of Many Common Nouns." *Proceedings of the National Academy of Sciences* 109: 3253–3258.

22  Newman, R. S., M. L. Rowe, and N. B. Ratner. 2015. "Input and Uptake at 7 Months Predicts Toddler Vocabulary: The Role of Child-Directed Speech and Infant Processing Skills in Language Development." *Journal of Child Language* 43: 1158–1173.

23  Meltzoff, A. N. 1995. "Understanding the Intentions of Others: Re-enactment of Intended Acts by 18-Month-Old Children." *Developmental Psychology* 31: 838–850.

24  McMurray, B. 2007. "Defusing the Childhood Vocabulary Explosion." *Science* 317: 631.

25  Baldwin, D. A. 1993. "Infants' Ability to Consult the Speaker for Clues to Word Reference." *Journal of Child Language* 20: 395–418.

26  Denham, S. A. 2019. "Emotional Competence During Childhood and Adolescence." In *Handbook of Emotional Development*, edited by V. LoBue, P. Pérez-Edgar, and K. Buss, 493–541. Cham, Switzerland: Springer.

27  Zeman, J., M. Cameron, and N. Price. 2019. "Sadness in Youth: Socialization, Regulation, and Adjustment." In *Handbook of Emotional Development*, edited by V. LoBue, P. Pérez-Edgar, and K. Buss, 227–256. Cham, Switzerland: Springer.

28  Drummond, J., E. F. Paul, W. E. Waugh, S. I. Hammond, and C. A. Brownell. 2014. "Here, There, and Everywhere: Emotion and Mental State Talk in Different Social Contexts Predicts Empathic Helping in Toddlers." *Frontiers in Psychology* 5: 361.

29  Piaget, J. 1947/1950. *La Psychologies de L'intelligence.* Translated by Malcolm Piercy and D. E. Berlyne. Oxford, England: Harcourt Brace.

30  Bergen, D., and D. Mauer. 2000. "Symbolic Play, Phonological Awareness, and Literacy Skills at Three Age Levels." In *Play and Literacy in Early Childhood: Research from Multiple Perspectives*, edited by K. A. Roskos and J. F. Christie, 45–62. Mahwah, NJ: Lawrence Erlbaum Associates Publishers.

31  Levy, A. K., L. Schaefer, and P. C. Phelps. 1986. "Increasing Preschool Effectiveness: Enhancing the Language Abilities of 3- and 4-Year-Old Children Through Planned Sociodramatic Play." *Early Childhood Research Quarterly* 1: 133–140.

32  Linsey, E. W., and M. J. Colwell. 2003. "Preschoolers' Emotional Competence: Links to Pretend and Physical Play." *Child Study Journal* 33: 39–53.

33  Weisberg, D. S., K. Hirsh-Pasek, and R. M. Golinkoff. 2013. "Guided Play: Where Curricular Goals Meet a Playful Pedagogy." *Mind, Brain, and Education* 7: 104–112.

34  Sorce, J. F., R. N. Emde, J. J. Campos, and M. D. Klinnert. 1985. "Maternal Emotional Signaling: Its Effect on the Visual Cliff Behavior of 1-Year-Olds." *Developmental Psychology* 21: 195–200.

35  Allan, N. P., L. E. Hume, D. M. Allan, A. L. Farrington, and C. J. Lonigan. 2014. "Relations Between Inhibitory Control and the Development of Academic Skills in Preschool and Kindergarten: A Meta-Analysis." *Developmental Psychology* 50: 2368–2379.

36  Duckworth, A. L., and M. E. Seligman. 2005. "Self-Discipline Outdoes IQ in Predicting Academic Performance of Adolescents." *Psychological Science* 16: 939–944.

37  Moffitt, T. E., L. Arseneault, D. Belsky, N. Dickson, R. J. Hancox, H. Harrington, R. Houts, R. Poulton, B. W. Roberts, S. Ross, and M. R. Sears. 2011. "A Gradient of Childhood Self-Control Predicts Health, Wealth, and Public Safety." *Proceedings of the National Academy of Sciences* 108: 2693–2698.

38  Galinsky, E. 2010. *Mind in the Making: The Seven Essential Life Skills Every Child Needs.* New York: Harper Studio.

39  Martins, E. C., A. Osório, M. Veríssimo, and C. Martins. 2016. "Emotion Understanding in Preschool Children: The Role of Executive Functions." *International Journal of Behavioral Development* 40(1): 1–10.

40  Mustich, E. September 13, 2013. "Cookie Monster Learns to Self-Regulate So Kids Can Too." *Huffington Post.* https://www.huffpost.com/entry/cookie-monster-self-regulation-sesame-street-rosemarie-truglio_n_3910334.

41  Mischel, W. 2014. *The Marshmallow Test: Understanding Self-Control and How to Master It.* New York: Random House.

42  Mischel, W., E. B. Ebbesen, and A. R. Zeiss. 1972. "Cognitive and Attentional Mechanisms in Delay of Gratification." *Journal of Personality and Social Psychology* 21: 204–218.

43  Shoda, Y., W. Mischel, and P. K. Peake. 1990. "Predicting Adolescent Cognitive and Self-Regulatory Competencies from Preschool Delay of Gratification: Identifying Diagnostic Conditions." *Developmental Psychology* 26: 978–986.

44  Ibid.

45  Bodrova, E., and D. Leong. 2006. *Tools of the Mind: The Vygotskian Approach to Early Childhood Education.* 2nd ed. Upper Saddle River, NJ: Pearson.

46  Blair, C., and C. C. Raver. 2014. "Closing the Achievement Gap Through Modification of Neurocognitive and Neuroendocrine Function: Results from a Cluster Randomized Controlled Trial of an Innovative Approach to the Education of Children in Kindergarten." *PloS One* 9(11): e112393.

47  Diamond, A., C. Lee, P. Senften, A. Lam, and D. Abbott. 2019. "Randomized Control Trial of Tools of the Mind: Marked Benefits to Kindergarten Children and Their Teachers." *PloS One* 14(9): e0222447.

48  Fivush, R., and N. R. Hammond. 1990. "Autobiographical Memory Across the Preschool Years: Toward Reconceptualizing Childhood Amnesia." In *Knowing and Remembering in Young Children*, edited by R. Fivush and J. A. Hudson, 223–248. New York: Cambridge University Press.

49  Nelson, K. 1992. "Emergence of Autobiographical Memory at Age 4." *Human Development* 35: 172–177.

50  Perner, J., and T. Ruffman. 1995. "Episodic Memory and Autonoetic Consciousness: Developmental Evidence and a Theory of Childhood Amnesia." *Journal of Experimental Child Psychology* 59: 516–548.

51  Povinelli, D., K. R. Landau, and H. K. Perilloux. 1996. "Self-Recognition in Young Children Using Delayed Versus Live Feedback: Evidence of a Developmental Asynchrony." *Child Development* 67: 1540–1554.

52 Gillespie, L. 2015. "Rocking and Rolling—It Takes Two: The Role of Co-Regulation in Building Self-Regulation Skills." *Young Children* 70: 94–96.

53 Vygotsky, L. S. 1978. *Mind in Society: The Development of Higher Mental Processes,* edited by M. Cole. Cambridge, MA: Harvard University Press. (Original work published 1930–1935.)

54 John-Steiner, V., and H. Mahn. 1996. "Sociocultural Approaches to Learning and Development: A Vygotskian Framework." *Educational Psychologist* 31: 191–206.

55 Bronfenbrenner, U., and P. Morris. 1998. "The Ecology of Developmental Processes." In *Handbook of Child Psychology* (vol. 1), edited by W. Damon. 5th ed. (New York: Wiley), 993–1028.

56 Goleman, D., and P. Senge. 2014. *The Triple Focus: A New Approach to Education.* Florence, MA: More Than Sound.

57 Armstrong, K. 2011. *Twelve Steps to a Compassionate Life.* New York: Alfred A Knopf.

58 Singer, T., and O. M. Klimecki. 2014. "Empathy and Compassion." *Current Biology* 24: 875–878.

59 Ibid.

60 Leiberg, S., O. Klimecki, and T. Singer. 2011. "Short-Term Compassion Training Increases Prosocial Behavior in a Newly Developed Prosocial Game." *PloS One* 6(3): e17798.

61 Weng, H. Y., A. S. Fox, A. J. Shackman, D. E. Stodola, J. Z. Caldwell, M. C. Olson ... and R. J. Davidson. 2013. "Compassion Training Alters Altruism and Neural Responses to Suffering." *Psychological Science* 24: 1171–1180.

62 Baumrind, D. 1967. "Child Care Practices Anteceding Three Patterns of Preschool Behavior." *Genetic Psychology Monographs* 75: 43–88.

63 Maccoby, E., and J. Martin. 1983. "Socialization in the Context of the Family: Parent-Child Interaction." In *Handbook of Child Psychology* (vol. 4), edited by P. H. Mussen and E. M. Hetherington, 1–101. New York: Wiley.

64 Hamlin, J. K., and K. Wynn. 2011. "Young Infants Prefer Prosocial to Antisocial Others." *Cognitive Development* 26: 30–39.

65 Goleman, D., and R. J. Davidson. 2017. *Altered Traits: Science Reveals How Meditation Changes Your Mind, Brain, and Body.* New York: Penguin.

66 Schonert-Reichl, K. A., E. Oberle, M. S. Lawlor, D. Abbott, K. Thomson, T. F. Oberlander, and A. Diamond. 2015. "Enhancing Cognitive and Social-Emotional Development Through a Simple-to-Administer Mindfulness-Based School Program for Elementary School Children: A Randomized Controlled Trial." *Developmental Psychology* 51: 52–66.

67 Zelazo, P. D., and K. E. Lyons. 2012. "The Potential Benefits of Mindfulness Training in Early Childhood: A Developmental Social Cognitive Neuroscience Perspective." *Child Development Perspectives* 6: 154–160.

68 Ibid.

69 Goldstein, J. 2003. *Insight Meditation: The Practice of Freedom.* Boulder, CO: Shambhala Publications.

70 Lin, X., W. Yang, L. Wu, L. Zhu, D. Wu, and H. Li. 2021. "Using an Inquiry-Based Science and Engineering Program to Promote Science Knowledge, Problem-Solving Skills, and Approaches to Learning in Preschool Children." *Early Education and Development* 32(5): 695–713.

71 Mills, C. M., C. H. Legare, M. Bills, and C. Mejias. 2010. "Preschoolers Use Questions as a Tool to Acquire Knowledge from Different Sources." *Journal of Cognition and Development* 11: 533–560.

72 Mills, C. M., and K. R. Sands. 2020. "Understanding Developmental and Individual Differences in the Process of Inquiry During the Preschool Years." In *The Questioning Child: Insights from Psychology and Education,* edited by L. P. Butler, S. Ronfard, and K. H. Corriveau, 144–163. New York: Cambridge University Press.

73 Chouinard, M. M. 2007. "Children's Questions: A Mechanism for Cognitive Development: IV. Children's Questions About Animals." *Monographs of the Society for Research in Child Development* 72: 58–82.

74 Jehn, K. A., and E. Mannix. 2001. "The Dynamic Nature of Conflict: A Longitudinal Study of Intragroup Conflict and Group Performance." *Academy of Management Journal* 44: 238–251.

75 Brownell, C. A., S. S. Iesue, S. R. Nichols, and M. Svetlova. 2013. "Mine or Yours? Development of Sharing in Toddlers in Relation to Ownership Understanding." *Child Development* 84: 906–920.

76 Hay, D. F. 2006. "Yours and Mine: Toddlers' Talk About Possessions with Familiar Peers." *British Journal of Developmental Psychology* 24: 39–52.

77 Brownell, C. A., S. S. Iesue, S. R. Nichols, and M. Svetlova. 2013. "Mine or Yours? Development of Sharing in Toddlers in Relation to Ownership Understanding." *Child Development* 84: 906–920.

78 Davidson, R. J., and S. Begley. 2013. *The Emotional Life of Your Brain: How Its Unique Patterns Affect the Way You Think, Feel, and Live—and How You Can Change Them.* New York: Penguin.

79 Hart, S., and V. Hodson. 2002. *The Compassionate Classroom: Relationship Based Teaching and Learning.* Encinitas, CA: Puddle Dancer Press.

# About the Author

**Rachael Katz, MS, Ed**, teaches social and emotional learning skills to parents and children. She has over twenty-five years of experience as an early childhood educator and school leader. Rachael was head of the Discovery School at the Bay Area Discovery Museum, head of social and emotional learning for Early Years at Dulwich College Beijing, and an elementary classroom teacher for preschool through third grade in public and private schools. In addition to working in school settings, Rachael has created and written television for Nick Jr. and Radio Television Hong Kong, and was a consultant for educational programs at Children's Television Workshop.

Rachael holds a master's degree in education from Bank Street College, and a BA from the Tisch School of the Arts at New York University.

**Helen Shwe Hadani, PhD**, is currently a fellow at the Brookings Institution where she conducts policy-focused research on the benefits of playful learning in both formal and informal contexts. Prior to joining Brookings, she served as director of research at the Bay Area Discovery Museum where she guided program and exhibit development. An expert in early childhood and creativity development, she has more than twenty years of experience in research and education settings, and has worked with toy, media, and technology companies, including Disney, Sesame Workshop, Apple, LEGO, Fisher-Price, and Mattel. Helen holds a BA in cognitive science from the University of Rochester, and a doctorate in psychology from Stanford University.

# Real change *is* possible

For more than forty-five years, New Harbinger has published proven-effective self-help books and pioneering workbooks to help readers of all ages and backgrounds improve mental health and well-being, and achieve lasting personal growth. In addition, our spirituality books offer profound guidance for deepening awareness and cultivating healing, self-discovery, and fulfillment.

Founded by psychologist Matthew McKay and Patrick Fanning, New Harbinger is proud to be an independent, employee-owned company. Our books reflect our core values of integrity, innovation, commitment, sustainability, compassion, and trust. Written by leaders in the field and recommended by therapists worldwide, New Harbinger books are practical, accessible, and provide real tools for real change.

 **newharbinger**publications

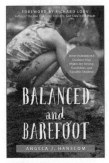
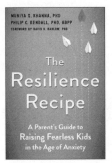